What are Oxford Literature Companions?

The Oxford Literature Companions (MFL) series is designed to provide you with comprehensive support for popular set texts. You can use the Companion alongside your novel, using relevant sections during your studies or using the book as a whole for revision.

Each Companion includes detailed guidance and practical activities on:

- **Plot and Structure**
- **Context**
- **Characters**
- **Language**
- **Themes**
- **Skills and Practice**

How does the book help with exam preparation?

As well as providing guidance on key areas of the novel, throughout this book you will also find 'Upgrade' features. These are tips to help with your exam preparation and performance.

In addition, the **Skills and Practice** chapter provides detailed guidance on areas such as how to prepare for the exam, understanding the question, planning your response and hints for what to do (or not do) in the exam. There is also a bank of **Sample questions** and **Sample answers**. The **Sample answers** are marked and include annotations and a summative comment.

How does this book help with terminology?

Throughout the book, key terms are highlighted in the text and explained on the same page with the equivalent term in French. The same terms are included in a detailed **Glossary** at the end of the book.

Which edition of this novel has been used?

Quotations have been taken from the Hachette (Livre de Poche) edition of *No et moi* (ISBN 9782253124801) © Editions Jean-Claude Lattès, 2007.

Contents

**MFL
AS/A Level**

No et moi

DELPHINE DE VIGAN

**Oxford
Literature
Companions**

...son

How does this book work?

Each book in the Oxford Literature Companions (MFL) series follows the same approach and includes the following features:

- **Key quotations** from the novel
- **Key terms** explained on the page in English with French translations, linked to a complete glossary at the end of the book
- **Activity boxes** with activities in French to help improve your understanding of the text and your language skills, including:
  - Vocabulary activities
  - Comprehension activities
  - Summary activities
  - Grammar activities
  - Translation activities
  - Research activities
- **Upgrade** tips to help prepare you for your assessment
- **Vocabulary and useful phrases** in French at the end of each chapter to aid your revision

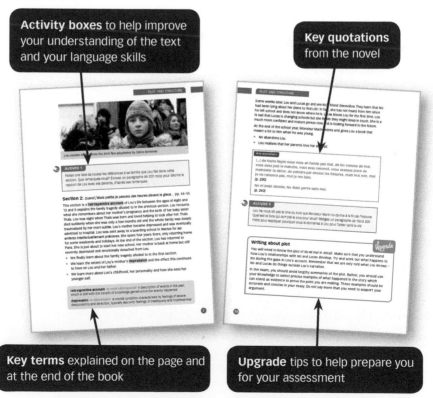

Activity boxes to help improve your understanding of the text and your language skills

Key quotations from the novel

Key terms explained on the page and at the end of the book

Upgrade tips to help prepare you for your assessment

Plot and Structure

Plot

Section 1: *Mademoiselle Bertignac, je ne vois pas votre nom...* pp. 11–43

The novel's main **protagonist** Lou begins her story at school, on the day when her teacher, Monsieur Marin, asks her for the topic of her class presentation (*exposé*). In a moment of panic, Lou decides that she will talk about the plight of homeless women in Paris. Her choice is inspired by a chance meeting with a homeless girl called No, some days earlier at the *gare d'Austerlitz*. Lou recalls her two previous meetings with No and describes the third meeting in which she asks No if she can interview her for her school project. As well as describing the beginnings of the unlikely friendship between Lou and No, this section also introduces us to Lucas, a classmate of Lou's. Lou describes her memories of the beginning of the school year when she joined the class. We begin to understand that Lou has no friends at school because she is younger than the other pupils, yet much cleverer. The most popular girls in the class, Axelle Vernoux and Léa Germain, are particularly spiteful towards her, whereas Lucas encourages her by smiling at her in class and talking to her at break: '**– T'inquiète pas, Pépite, je suis sûr que tout va bien se passer'** (*p. 38*). This section shows us that Lou sees herself as a shy and clumsy misfit: '**D'où vient qu'avec un Q.I. de 160 je ne suis pas foutue de faire un lacet?'** (*p. 13*). Her classmates, on the other hand, see her as a haughty and swotty teacher's pet. Several comments made by Lou in this section suggest that her home life is more troubled than her classmates and teachers know.

● Lou's **narrative voice** encourages the reader to **empathise** with her.

● The reader begins to suspect that Lou may be hiding a family secret or tragedy from us.

● Vigan communicates key details about the characters of Lou, No and Lucas.

> **Key quotations**
>
> – Je vais retracer l'itinéraire d'une jeune femme sans abri, sa vie, enfin... son histoire. Je veux dire... comment elle se retrouve dans la rue.
> (*p. 12*)
>
> Ma mère ne sort plus de chez moi depuis des années et mon père pleure en cachette dans la salle de bains.
> (*p. 14*)

protagonist *le / la protagoniste* the central character in a story

narrative voice *la voix narrative* the voice of the person who is telling the story

empathise with someone *s'identifier avec quelqu'un* to understand someone's point of view or to feel a connection with someone

Lou outside school, from the 2010 film adaptation by Zabou Breitman

Activité 1

Faites une liste de toutes les références à sa famille que Lou fait dans cette section. Que remarquez-vous? Écrivez un paragraphe de 200 mots pour décrire le rapport de Lou avec ses parents, d'après ses remarques.

Section 2: *Quand j'étais petite je passais des heures devant la glace...* pp. 44–55

This section is a **retrospective account** of Lou's life between the ages of eight and 13 and it explains the family tragedy alluded to in the previous section. Lou recounts what she remembers about her mother's pregnancy and the birth of her baby sister Thaïs. Lou was eight when Thaïs was born and loved helping to look after her. Thaïs died suddenly when she was only a few months old and the whole family was deeply traumatised by her *mort subite*. Lou's mother became depressed and was eventually admitted to hospital. Lou was sent away to a boarding school in Nantes for *les enfants intellectuellement précoces*. She spent four years there, only returning home for some weekends and holidays. At the end of the section, Lou has returned to Paris. She is just about to start her new school. Her mother is back at home but still severely depressed and emotionally detached from Lou.

- We finally learn about the family tragedy alluded to in the first section.
- We learn the extent of Lou's mother's **depression** and the effect this continues to have on Lou and her father.
- We learn more about Lou's childhood, her personality and how she sees her younger self.

retrospective account *le récit rétrospectif* a description of events in the past which is told with the benefit of knowledge gained since the events happened

depression *la dépression* a mental condition characterised by feelings of severe despondency and dejection, typically also with feelings of inadequacy and hopelessness

> **Key quotation**
>
> **Ma mère est tombée malade. Nous l'avons vue s'éloigner, petit à petit, sans pouvoir la retenir, nous avons tendu la main sans pouvoir la toucher, nous avons crié sans qu'elle semble nous entendre.**
> *(p. 50)*

> **Activité 2**
>
> En vous servant des descriptions dans cette partie, écrivez des phrases qui décrivent la mère de Lou avant et après le décès de Thaïs. Par exemple: avant elle était gaie; après elle était triste.
> *(40–50 mots)*

Section 3: *Je compte une, deux, trois, quatre gouttes… pp. 56–72*

In this section, we return to the present. Lou takes up her story where she left it at the end of Section 1. At the beginning of Section 3, Lou is taking medicine to reduce her **insomnia**. Sometimes her head is so full of thoughts that she cannot sleep. Lou is worried about her *exposé* which is approaching. She also remembers how nice Lucas has been to her recently.

Lou thinks back to her recent meetings with No. No has agreed to be interviewed and Lou meets her several times a week after school to ask her questions. No introduces Lou to some of her acquaintances: Momo, Michel and Roger. Lou buys No drinks in a bar by the station and No begins to tell Lou about her life. We learn that No does not have a place to live. Every day she must find somewhere to sleep that night; sometimes she gets a place in a homeless shelter, sometimes she shares a friend's tent. Lou's descriptions of their meetings reveal No's personality to the reader. She is defensive and secretive about her own life but enjoys hearing about Lou's days at school. In this section we notice that No smokes and drinks as much as she can but hardly eats anything. She is dirty, tired and very thin: **'je vois la fatigue sur son visage, c'est comme un voile gris qui la recouvre, l'enveloppe, et peut-être la protège'** *(p. 60)*.

At the end of the section Lou does her presentation. She gets 18 out of 20 for it and is so exhausted afterwards that she falls asleep in class.

- Vigan uses No's conversations with Lou to provide a detailed insight into the life of a homeless woman in Paris.
- Lou's friendships with No and Lucas develop.

> **insomnia** *l'insomnie (f)* problems getting to sleep or staying asleep

> **Key quotation**
>
> **Nous prenons rendez-vous d'une fois sur l'autre, parfois elle vient, parfois elle ne vient pas. J'y pense toute la journée, j'attends la fin des cours avec impatience, dès que la sonnerie retentit je me précipite dans le métro, avec toujours cette peur de ne pas la revoir, cette peur qu'il lui soit arrivé quelque chose.**
>
> *(p. 58)*

Activité 3

Lisez les propos de No sur sa vie à la rue. En utilisant les détails donnés par No, créez une présentation PowerPoint sur la vie d'un SDF à Paris. Faites des recherches sur Internet pour trouver plus de renseignements sur les sans-abri en France. Dans un paragraphe écrit, comparez les expériences de No avec d'autres témoignages. Que remarquez-vous?

Section 4: *J'y suis retournée à l'heure dite, le jour dit...* pp. 73–99

It is the Tuesday after Lou's *exposé*. She goes back to the station to see No as agreed but No has vanished. Just before the Christmas break, Lucas surprises Lou by inviting her round to his flat. Lou panics, refuses and immediately regrets her decision. Lou spends her Christmas holidays thinking about No and Lucas. She wishes she had done more to help No and wonders how things would be different if people helped each other more. The death of Mouloud, a homeless man who lived on the street near her home, makes her think about injustice and **hypocrisy**. Her neighbours leave flowers and candles at the spot where Mouloud used to sleep but none of them made an effort to help him when he was alive: '**Les chiens on peut les prendre chez soi, mais pas les SDF**' *(p. 81)*. Lou also resents her parents' hypocritical behaviour. At Christmas they pretend to have a good time purely for the sake of tradition: '**nous serions sans doute tous d'accord pour conclure que cela n'a pas de sens, mais personne ne le dit, alors chaque année le carton est ouvert, le sapin décoré, le menu prévu à l'avance**' *(p. 83)*. Lou hates the idea that she is living in a separate world from No. She spends her holidays travelling around Paris looking for her and finally finds her at a soup kitchen, where they have a huge argument. No sends her away and Lou feels even more lonely than usual. When she goes back to school, Lucas asks her out again. Her social awkwardness and shyness mean that she once again refuses.

- Lou's idealistic approach to justice and social equality is demonstrated.
- The friendship between Lou and Lucas develops further; Lou begins to wonder what it might be like to kiss Lucas.

hypocrisy *l'hypocrisie (f)* claiming to have standards while not actually living up to those standards

Activité 4

Imaginez que vous observez la discussion entre No et Lou devant la soupe populaire de la rue Clément *(pp. 92–93)*. Faites une liste des différences entre No et Lou. Utilisez les verbes 'avoir' et 'être' pour vous aider. Par exemple:

- No n'a pas d'argent; Lou a un sac à dos de marque.
- No est sale; Lou est triste.
  (40–50 mots)

Key quotation

Je suis descendue dans le métro, j'ai attendu la rame, je regardais les affiches et j'avais envie de pleurer parce que No n'était plus là, parce que je l'avais laissée partir, parce que je ne lui avais pas dit merci.
(p. 74)

Section 5: *Je sors par la grande porte...* pp. 100–129

No reappears one day outside Lou's school as Lou is going home. Despite the astonished looks of her classmates, Lou takes No to a bar. She is pleased to see her, but quickly becomes worried about her. No seems to have changed a lot since they last saw each other: **'De loin ça se voit qu'elle est sale, son jean est maculé de traînées noires, ses cheveux collés par petits paquets'** *(p. 100)*. After hearing about how hard No is finding life on the streets, Lou decides to ask her parents to let No stay with them. She prepares a carefully structured set of arguments, just like she has learnt at school. To her great surprise, they agree.

The next time she sees No waiting for her after school she decides to ask Lucas for help. She quickly introduces No to Lucas and explains that she needs to get No cleaned up so that she can make a good first impression on Lou's parents. In this scene, Lou shows a new decisive side. In contrast, No has no energy and is sick as soon as they get to Lucas's flat. She tells Lou she has taken pills of some kind. She passively lets Lou and Lucas look after her: **'Elle n'a plus la force. Plus la force de protester, plus la force de dire non'** *(p. 111)*. Together they give No a bath and find her some clean clothes. Lou is touched by Lucas's unquestioning generosity and helpfulness. This episode creates a stronger connection between them because No becomes their shared secret.

Lou takes No home with her. Lou's parents are polite if distant with No, and after a rather awkward meal they get Thaïs's old room ready for No to sleep in. No begins to settle into her new existence. She gradually spends more time with the family and joins in with chores and meal times.

After spending a few weeks recovering her strength, No begins to look for a job. No and Lou spend a lot of time with Lucas after school. They go to his flat to listen to music.

- The relationships between No and Lou, and Lou and Lucas, develop.
- The importance of No as a catalyst for change in Lou's family is seen as her parents take the small but significant step of allowing No to sleep in Thaïs's room.
- We see Lou becoming more confident at school, again due in part to her friendship with No.

Activité 5

a) Traduisez le paragraphe suivant en anglais.

Pendant des semaines elle a pris sa place dans des files d'attente pour manger, laver ses vêtements, pour obtenir un lit, ici ou là. Pendant des semaines elle a dormi avec ses chaussures planquées sous son oreiller, ses sacs coincés entre elle et le mur, son argent et sa carte d'identité dans sa culotte, pour ne pas se les faire voler. Elle a dormi sur le qui-vive, dans des draps en papier, sous des couvertures de fortune ou avec son blouson pour seule protection. Pendant des semaines elle s'est retrouvée dehors au petit matin, sans projet, sans perspective. Elle a erré des journées entières, dans ce monde parallèle qui est pourtant le nôtre, elle n'a cherché rien d'autre qu'un endroit dont elle ne serait pas virée, un endroit pour s'asseoir ou pour dormir.
(p. 119)

b) Dans ce paragraphe, Lou utilise certains mots plusieurs fois pour influencer le lecteur. Faites une liste des mots et expressions les plus répétés. Écrivez une phrase de 20 à 30 mots pour expliquer l'effet de cette répétition sur le lecteur.

Key quotations

Il y a moi. En face d'elle. Quelque chose me retient. Alors je remarque ses yeux gonflés, les traces sombres sur son visage, son incertitude, d'un seul coup je n'ai plus d'amertume, ni de ressentiment, seulement l'envie de la prendre dans mes bras. Je traverse. Je dis viens.
(p. 100)

Je ne sais pas ce qu'elle a avalé, elle est là sans y être, elle ne proteste pas non plus quand je lui explique que nous allons chez moi, que mes parents sont d'accord et nous attendent.
(pp. 113–114)

Section 6: *Sur les conseils de mon père, No est retournée voir l'assistante sociale qui s'occupe d'elle...* pp. 130–169

No is becoming more settled at Lou's place. She starts working as a **chambermaid** in a hotel and she becomes more relaxed around Lou's parents. She begins to confide in Lou and her mother and tells them about her childhood. No and Lou spend more and more time with Lucas at his flat; these moments are precious for Lou. For the first time in her life she has friends she can spend time with.

When Lou's father is away in China for work, her mother lets them stay up late and drink wine. She tells No stories about Lou's childhood and even begins to talk about Thaïs. After a few weeks at work No seems increasingly unhappy. Lou catches her stealing medicine from the bathroom cabinet and throwing up in the toilet.

No decides that she wants to go and visit her mother in Ivry. One Sunday, Lou tells her parents they are going to the flea market. Instead they go to the council estate where No's mother now lives with No's half-brother. No is nervous. When they get to the flat, her mother refuses to speak to them and will not even open the door to them. Lou can tell No is angry and upset, but No refuses to talk about the incident.

- We learn how hard it is for No to find and keep a job in Paris.
- We learn about No's family, particularly her mother, and what life was like for No when she was growing up.
- Lou's mother becomes more engaged with other members of the family, particularly Lou's father; in contrast, No's mother rejects her daughter.

Activité 6

Mettez ces événements dans la vie de No dans le bon ordre.

a) La grand-mère de No est morte. ☐

b) No a été placée dans une famille d'accueil. ☐

c) No est née en Normandie. ☐

d) No a rencontré Loïc. ☐

e) No est entrée au collège. ☐

f) No est allée vivre avec sa mère et l'homme à la moto. ☐

g) No a été élevée par ses grands-parents. ☐

h) L'homme à la moto est parti. ☐

i) No a été envoyée dans un internat éducatif. ☐

j) No et sa mère ont déménagé pour s'installer à Ivry. ☐

chambermaid *la femme de chambre* a maid who cleans bedrooms and bathrooms in a hotel

> **Key quotation**
>
> Dans la queue de la cantine j'ai pensé à ma mère, à la mobilité de son visage et de ses mains, à sa voix qui n'est plus un murmure. Peu importe qu'il y ait ou non une explication, une relation de cause à effet. Elle va mieux, elle est en train de retrouver le goût de la parole et de la compagnie et rien d'autre ne doit compter.
> *(p. 158)*

Section 7: *Le mari de ma tante Sylvie a rencontré une nouvelle femme, il veut divorcer...* pp. 170–192

Lou and her parents are planning to leave Paris for a few days during Lou's February half-term break. The evening before they leave, No and Lou go to Lucas's flat. Lou is anxious about leaving No and No seems worried about being on her own. Towards the end of the week, No stops answering the phone when Lou's father rings to check on her. During the return journey Lou becomes increasingly worried about No. She is convinced that something terrible has happened to her. When they get home, No is not there. They find empty vodka bottles and medicine packets in her bedroom.

When No finally comes home, Lou's father has a serious talk with her that Lou is not allowed to listen to. No has begun to work night shifts. She sleeps all day and works all night. She is changing. She becomes more secretive and stops keeping her appointments with her social worker. Lou's father warns her that if she wants to live in their home she must follow their rules and not put Lou in danger. On the first day of the new term, Lou's father tells Lou that No needs more help than they can give her. He wants her to go to a centre where she will get the help she needs. Rather than going back to an institution, No packs her bags, cleans her room and disappears when everyone is out.

- No's behaviour changes.
- Lou realises that life is more complicated that her idealistic version of it had led her to believe.
- The events of this section show that No's problems are not simply solved by having somewhere to live: being 'homeless' is about more than not having somewhere to call 'home'.

> **Activité 7**
>
> Imaginez que vous êtes le père de Lou. Écrivez une liste de règles pour No. Commencez chaque règle soit par 'il faut...', soit par un verbe à l'impératif.
> Par exemple: il faut rentrer avant minuit.

> **Key quotation**
>
> Elle ne vient plus dans la cuisine, ni dans le salon, se faufile dans la salle de bains quand elle est sûre de ne croiser personne. Le soir elle dîne avec nous avant de repartir à l'hôtel, c'est la même scène qu'il y a un mois, la même lumière, les mêmes places, les mêmes gestes, vues de haut les images pourraient se confondre, se superposer, mais de là où je suis on peut percevoir combien l'air a changé, s'est alourdi.
> *(p. 186)*

Section 8: *No a sonné à la porte…* pp. 193–227

No moves into Lucas's flat and Lou and Lucas try to look after her in secret. But No is drinking more and more and still working nights. She is often ill or asleep during the day. Meanwhile, Lou's parents are redecorating the spare room and making plans for holidays. Lou's mother is even thinking about going back to work. Lou hates the way they seem to have forgotten No and are getting on with their lives as if she had never been there.

Lucas tries to be strict with No. He pours her bottles of vodka down the sink and refuses to give her a key to his flat. Lou notices that No suddenly has enough money to buy her own drinks. She also sees unexplained marks on No's body. Lou never suggests what these marks might be but her descriptions of No's new-found wealth together with her increased reliance on drugs and alcohol lead the reader to suspect that No might be getting paid for sex at the hotel.

One evening, Lou and No see No's homeless friend Momo begging on the street. He refuses the money that No tries to give him. No tells Lou about her childhood sweetheart Loïc. She is saving money to go to Ireland to find him. Lucas begins to realise that he and Lou are not strong enough to look after No: 'il dit nous n'allons pas y arriver, Lou, il faut que tu comprennes, on ne peut pas la laisser dans cet état, elle prend des trucs, on ne peut plus lui parler, on ne peut pas se battre contre ça' *(p. 206)*. Lou refuses to give up on No. She is angry with Lucas for flirting with the other girls in the class and with her parents for forgetting about No.

- No's unpredictable behaviour puts a strain on the relationship between Lucas and Lou.
- Lou resents her parents' behaviour and feels abandoned by them; she keeps secrets from them and spends most of her time at Lucas's home.

> **Key quotations**
>
> Je n'aime pas cette nouvelle vie. Je n'aime pas quand *les choses* s'effacent, se perdent, je n'aime pas faire semblant d'avoir oublié. Je n'oublie pas.
> *(p. 211)*
>
> Il y a par exemple que moi aussi j'en ai marre, marre, marre d'être toute seule, marre qu'elle me parle comme si j'étais la fille de la gardienne, marre des mots et des expériences, marre de tout. Il y a que je voudrais qu'elle me regarde comme les autres mères regardent leurs enfants, […].
> *(p. 220)*

Activité 8

Imaginez que Lucas poste des mises à jour sur Twitter pour informer Lou de l'état actuel de No. Mettez-vous à la place de Lucas. Composez une série de trois tweets pour indiquer comment va No pendant une semaine. Attention: ne dépassez pas les 140 caractères autorisés!

> **Lucas M** ✦ @Lucas123
> No n'est pas rentrée. 😞

> **Lucas M** ✦ @Lucas123
> Je m'inquiète pour elle. Lou aussi

Section 9: *Avant de rencontrer No, je croyais que la violence était dans les cris…* pp. 228–250

Lou's parents discover not only that No is living at Lucas's home, but also that Lucas lives there alone. Lou's father is furious with Lou for lying to him. Lou is furious with them for abandoning No. Lou tries to explain why No doesn't want to go back to a centre. No needs to move out of Lucas's flat and Lou decides to go with her. She packs a bag and runs away from home. No treats Lou to an extravagant day in Paris and they spend the night at a seedy hotel.

The following day, they go to the station to catch the train to Ireland. While No goes to buy the tickets, Lou sits in the waiting room. After a while, Lou realises that No has disappeared. No explanation is given for No's decision to abandon Lou. Lou waits for No all day before returning home to her worried parents. She is touched by her mother's tears.

Some weeks later, Lou and Lucas go and see No's friend Geneviève. They learn that No had been lying about her plans to find Loïc: in fact, she has not heard from him since he left school and does not know where he is. Lucas kisses Lou for the first time. Lou is sad that Lucas is changing schools but she thinks they might keep in touch. She is a much more confident and mature person now and is looking forward to the future.

At the end of the school year, Monsieur Marin retires and gives Lou a book that meant a lot to him when he was young.

- No abandons Lou.
- Lou realises that her parents love her after all.

Key quotations

[...] de toute façon vous vous en foutez pas mal, de No comme de moi, vous avez jeté le manche, vous avez renoncé, vous essayez juste de maintenir le décor, de peindre par-dessus les fissures, mais moi non, moi je ne renonce pas, moi je me bats.
(p. 230)

No m'avait laissée, No était partie sans moi.
(p. 243)

Activité 9

Lou ne nous dit pas le titre du livre que Monsieur Marin lui donne à la fin de l'histoire. Quel est le livre qui compte le plus pour vous? Rédigez un paragraphe de 150 à 200 mots pour expliquer pourquoi vous le donneriez à Lou pour l'aider dans la vie.

Writing about plot

You will need to know the plot of *No et moi* in detail. Make sure that you understand how Lou's relationships with No and Lucas develop. Try and work out what happens to No during the gaps in Lou's account. Remember that we are only told what Lou knows – No and Lucas do things outside Lou's narration.

In the exam, you should avoid lengthy summaries of the plot. Rather, you should use your knowledge to select precise examples of what happened in the story which can stand as evidence to prove the point you are making. These examples should be accurate and concise in your essay. Do not say more than you need to support your argument.

Structure

The novel is a **first-person narrative** and the **narrator** is 13-year-old Lou Bertignac. Lou's narrative is divided into 55 short chapters. The effect of these short chapters is to make the novel seem like a diary; the events appear very immediate and we therefore feel as if we are getting an intimate account of Lou's thoughts. The action of the novel spans most of a school year, from late October to early July. Lou is retelling her story from a point after it has ended. She uses a combination of the perfect tense (*le passé composé*) and the present tense (*le présent*) to describe her life during this period. Lou intersperses this story of her friendship with No with descriptions of events that happened before she met No.

She uses a combination of the perfect, the pluperfect (*le plus-que-parfait*) and the imperfect (*l'imparfait*) tenses to recount events that happened before the beginning of this story.

> **first person narrative** *le récit à la première personne* a story told from the perspective of a narrator speaking directly about himself or herself, using the pronoun 'I' / *je*
>
> **narrator** *le narrateur / la narratrice* the person who is telling the story

Activité 10

a) Relisez cette description du jour de la rentrée. Identifiez le temps de chaque verbe souligné: choisissez entre l'imparfait, le passé composé et le plus-que-parfait.

> Je ne <u>connaissais</u> personne et j'<u>avais</u> peur. Je <u>m'étais installée</u> dans le fond, Monsieur Marin <u>distribuait</u> les fiches. Lucas <u>s'est tourné</u> vers moi, il <u>m'a souri</u>. Les fiches <u>étaient</u> vertes.
> (p. 21)

b) Relisez cet extrait de la page suivante du roman (*p. 22*). Identifiez le temps utilisé.

> Aujourd'hui je connais tous les noms, les prénoms et les habitudes de la classe, les affinités et les rivalités, le rire de Léa Germain et les chuchotements d'Axelle, les jambes interminables de Lucas qui dépassent dans les allées [...].
> (p. 22)

c) Comparez les deux extraits dans un paragraphe de 100 mots.

Narrative time

Although Lou tells much of her story in the present tense, she is in fact writing a **retrospective narrative**. When she begins the story she already knows how it will end. This is revealed when she comments on the action from within it. For example, in Section 6, she describes happy memories of No but hints that this will not always be the case.

Key quotation

Quoi qu'il arrive, plus tard quand je penserai à elle, je sais que ces images l'emporteront, lumineuses, intenses, son visage ouvert, son rire avec Lucas, le bonnet de laine que mon père lui a offert enfoncé sur ses cheveux en bataille, ces moments où elle est sans doute elle-même, sans peur et sans rancœur, ses yeux brillants dans le halo bleu de la télévision.
(p. 140)

The crisis which Lou predicts in this quotation happens at the beginning of Section 7 when No begins drinking heavily and working nights at the hotel. After Lou and her parents return from holiday to find empty vodka bottles in No's room, the action of the novel speeds up until it reaches its conclusion or ***denouement*** in Section 9. Here, Lou's parents discover that Lou and Lucas have been hiding No, which in turn leads to No's disappearance, Lucas's move to his mother's flat and Lou's increased maturity and self-confidence. 'Denouement' comes from the French word 'le dénouement', which means untying or untangling. It comes from the verb 'dénouer', to untie.

retrospective narrative *le récit rétrospectif* a story in which the narrator describes events looking back from a point in time after the end of the story has been reached

denouement *le dénouement* the story's conclusion

Activité 11

Dans le dénouement du roman, Lou nous explique la situation finale de Lucas: **'L'an prochain Lucas ira vivre avec sa mère à Neuilly, ils vendront l'appartement'** *(p. 248)*. Écrivez une phrase pour décrire le destin de chaque personnage.

Activité 12

a) Mettez ces événements dans l'ordre dans lequel ils se passent dans la vie de Lou.

a) Lou est allée dans un collège spécialisé à Nantes. ☐ ☐

b) Lou a rencontré No. ☐ ☐

c) Lou a présenté No à Lucas. ☐ ☐

d) Lou est partie en vacances avec ses parents. ☐ ☐

e) La sœur de Lou est née. ☐ ☐

f) Lou a attendu No dans la salle d'attente. ☐ ☐

g) La mère de Lou est sortie de l'hôpital. ☐ ☐

h) No est partie de chez Lou. ☐ ☐

i) Lucas a embrassé Lou. ☐ ☐

j) La mère de Lou est tombée enceinte. ☐ ☐

k) Lou a eu 18 sur 20 pour son exposé. ☐ ☐

l) Les parents de Lou ont découvert la vérité sur No et Lucas. ☐ ☐

m) La sœur de Lou est morte. ☐ ☐

n) Lou est rentrée au lycée. ☐ ☐

o) No est arrivée chez Lucas. ☐ ☐

p) Monsieur Marin a donné son livre à Lou. ☐ ☐

q) No s'est installée chez Lou. ☐ ☐

r) Lou est retournée à Paris. ☐ ☐

s) Lou a décidé de faire son exposé sur les sans-abri. ☐ ☐

t) Lou s'est enfuie de chez elle. ☐ ☐

u) No a trouvé un travail. ☐ ☐

v) Lou a demandé à ses parents d'héberger No. ☐ ☐

b) Maintenant mettez cette même liste dans l'ordre où Lou raconte les événements dans le récit. Que remarquez-vous? Écrivez un paragraphe de 200 mots pour expliquer la différence entre l'ordre vécu et l'ordre raconté.

Writing about structure

Upgrade

The structural decisions an author makes are relevant to help answer a range of exam questions. For example, think about how the order of events described by Lou helps to create a fuller picture of the characters: what does Lou's parents' first meeting with No in Section 5 tell us about how Lou's mother has changed since Lou first refers to her in Section 1? Why do you think Lou waits until Section 2 before revealing her family's secret to the reader? How do the revelations in Section 2 change how we feel about what happens in Section 1?

Think too about why Vigan might have decided to include some events in the novel. For example, why does Vigan describe the two occasions on which Lou meets Momo? Why does she include the description of Mouloud's death in Section 4 and the visit to Ivry in Section 6?

Consider how Vigan's choice of narrative voice and the chronological order of the events involving No may help involve the reader in the story by building tension as events progress and ensuring the reader's continued engagement as they wait to see how the story will end.

Lou and No wait for the train to Ireland. The difference in their expressions suggests that something unexpected is about to happen.

Vocabulary

l'amertume (f) bitterness

se battre contre quelque chose to fight against something

un enfant intellectuellement précoce an intellectually advanced or gifted child

l'exposé (m) class presentation

être en grave dépression to be severely depressed

la famille d'accueil foster family

héberger quelqu'un to take someone in, shelter someone

l'hypocrisie (f) hypocrisy

s'identifier avec quelqu'un to empathise with someone

insomniaque insomniac, having trouble sleeping

les médicaments (m) medicine

la mort subite sudden death, especially of a baby

le passé composé the perfect (tense)

le personnage character (in a novel)

le plus-que-parfait the pluperfect (tense)

QI (quotient intellectuel) IQ

la relation de cause à effet cause-and-effect relationship

le ressentiment resentment

les sans-abri (m) homeless people

les SDF (sans domicile fixe) (m) homeless people

la soupe populaire soup kitchen

le temps tense

tomber enceinte to get / become pregnant

Useful phrases

Le roman est un récit écrit à la première personne The novel is written in the first person

Le lecteur entend la voix narrative de Lou The reader hears Lou's narrative voice

Il faut faire la différence entre l'auteur et la narratrice We must distinguish between the author and the narrator

le développement de l'intrigue the unfolding of the plot

Contrairement à ce qui se passe au début du roman,... Unlike what happens at the beginning of the novel,...

Par contre, dans la prochaine section... By contrast, in the next section...

Comme nous voyons au début / au milieu / dans le dénouement du roman... As we see at the beginning / middle / end of the novel...

Les événements du roman se déroulent... The events of the novel take place...

Le récit est focalisé sur... The plot focuses on....

Dès le début... Right from the beginning...

À plusieurs reprises... At several recurring points...

Au fur et à mesure que l'histoire se développe... As the storyline develops...

Les dernières pages nous laissent un sentiment de... The final pages leave us with a feeling of...

capter l'intérêt (m) du lecteur to capture the reader's interest

Biography of Delphine de Vigan

- Delphine de Vigan is a French novelist and playwright.
- Vigan was born in 1966 in Boulogne-Billancourt, a wealthy suburb to the west of Paris.
- To date, she has written seven novels and several screenplays.
- *No et moi*, her fourth novel, was published in 2007. It was written between May 2006 and March 2007.
- She wrote the novel to draw public attention to the increasing number of homeless women she was seeing on the streets of Paris.
- It was awarded two prizes: the prestigious French *prix des libraires* (2008) and the Rotary International Prize (2009).
- The success of *No et moi* meant that Vigan could give up her day-job at an advertising agency and become a full-time professional novelist.
- *No et moi* has been translated into 20 languages and it was adapted for the cinema in 2010 by Zabou Breitman.

Delphine de Vigan

- In 2016 Vigan was awarded the *ordre des Arts et des Lettres*, which might be described as the French equivalent of the OBE.
- Vigan's other novels are: *Jours sans faim* (2001) (under the pseudonym Lou Delvig); *Les jolis garçons* (2005); *Un soir de décembre* (2005); *Les heures souterraines* (2009); *Rien ne s'oppose à la nuit* (2011); and *D'après une histoire vraie* (2015).

Upgrade

Knowing the context of the novel will help to make your answers more insightful. However, you should only mention the author's background in relation to how it may have affected what Delphine de Vigan shows in the novel.

Historical and cultural context

No et moi is set in Paris. The exact year is not specified but it is probably set during the academic year 2005–2006. In the mid-2000s, riots in the Parisian **suburbs** revealed a split in French society between the rich and the poor, and between the white French majority and North- and West-African ethnic minorities.

Genre

As well as being a first-person narrative, *No et moi* is a modern take on a **bildungsroman**, or coming-of-age story. Through Lou's words and actions, we see her grow up from a shy and insecure child to a confident and articulate young woman.

Activité 1

Un bildungsroman est l'histoire d'une progression de l'enfance ou l'adolescence à l'âge adulte. Écrivez un paragraphe pour expliquer à quel point la vie d'un(e) adolescent(e) est différente de la vie d'un(e) adulte dans *No et moi*.

Setting

Lou's exact address is never specified but on p. 27 she tells No that she lives near *Filles du Calvaire* metro station, not far from the *Cirque d'hiver*. This suggests that she lives in the 11ᵗʰ **arrondissement** of Paris, between *place de la Bastille* and *place de la République*. This is a middle-class area of the city where many families and young people live. Without being ostentatiously wealthy, her family are well-off enough to be able to buy her books and a computer. They live in a three-bedroom flat in a central part of Paris. Lou appears to have led a sheltered, middle-class life where she has not known hunger or poverty. She attends a school (*lycée*) for mainly well-to-do students in central Paris.

suburbs *le banlieue* district on the outskirts of a large city. Although wealthy suburbs exist in France, the word *banlieue* often implies an area of poverty and social exclusion

bildungsroman *le bildungsroman* a German word (also used in French and English) for a novel which describes the emotional and intellectual development of a hero, usually as they move from childhood or adolescence to adulthood

arrondissement *l'arrondissement (m)* a section of central Paris: Paris is divided up into 20 *arrondissements*, rather as London is divided into boroughs such as Westminster and Chelsea. The lower the *arrondissement* number, the closer it is to the centre of Paris

Her classmates have enough money to go to the café after school and to buy branded clothing. Throughout the novel, Vigan contrasts the oppressive atmosphere of Lou's home with the much freer and more relaxed atmosphere of Lucas's flat.

She also contrasts the warm and cosy homes of Lou and Lucas with the cold streets where No lives.

Key quotations

Plus tard nous écoutons des chansons, avachis dans le canapé, la fumée des cigarettes nous enveloppe d'un nuage opaque, le temps s'arrête, il me semble que les guitares nous protègent, que le monde nous appartient.
(p. 129)

Dehors des femmes et des hommes dorment enfouis dans des sacs de couchage ou sous des cartons vides, au-dessus des bouches de métro, sous les ponts, ou à même le sol, dehors des femmes et des hommes dorment dans les recoins d'une ville dont ils sont exclus.
(p. 125)

Lou avoids spending time on her own at home with her parents. Instead she likes going to the *gare d'Austerlitz* after school and this is where she meets No. The *gare d'Austerlitz* is one of Paris's six large terminus railway stations. It is on the Left Bank (the south side of the river Seine) near the *Jardin des Plantes* and serves the central and south-west regions of France. Lou uses the Paris underground (*métro*) to get there. Lou and No spend time in a café by the station, the *Relais d'Auvergne*. At the end of the novel, No abandons Lou at another Parisian terminus station, the *gare St-Lazare*.

Large stations are appealing places for both No and Lou to spend time. No feels safe because she can hide among the crowds of passers-by. Lou likes watching the behaviour of the travellers who arrive and leave. She finds an emotional connection with these strangers' feelings which she does not experience with her parents at home. The station also represents the friendship between No and Lou. On the one hand, as a place of transience and constant movement, it is as chaotic and unpredictable as No's life on the streets. On the other hand, the regularity and reliability of the train timetable represents Lou's highly routine-focused existence.

Large stations are appealing places for both No and Lou

The name of Lou's school is not mentioned in the novel. But Lou's references to the Bar Botté, where students go after school, suggests that Vigan has probably based Lou's school on a real school: the lycée Hélène Boucher in the 20th *arrondissement*, which is just opposite a bar of the same name. These references to identifiable places add a note of reality to the novel which makes the events it depicts feel more believable.

Activité 2

Regardez le plan de Paris ci-dessous ou trouvez un autre plan en ligne. Pour chaque endroit mentionné dans le roman, écrivez une phrase pour décrire sa position géographique. Par exemple: Le lycée de Lou se trouve à l'est de Paris.

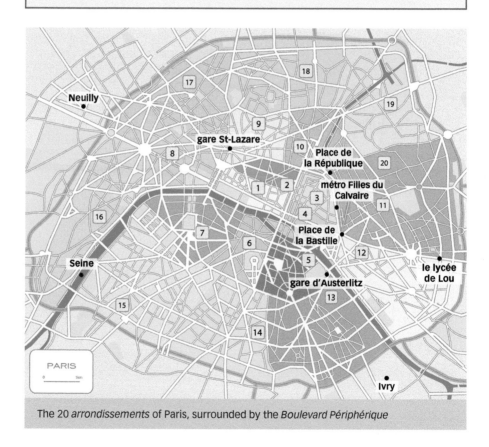

The 20 *arrondissements* of Paris, surrounded by the *Boulevard Périphérique*

The French education system

In France, education is compulsory between the ages of six and 16, but in practice many children go to nursery school (*l'école maternelle*) before they begin primary school at six (*l'école élémentaire*) and most French pupils stay at school until they are 18.

The French system allows pupils to move one or two years ahead (*sauter des classes*) if they are more intellectually advanced than their peers. This is the case for Lou, who skips the first year of elementary school (CP) and then the penultimate year (CM1) two years later. This means that by the time she gets to the **lycée** where the story is set, she is two years younger than most of the other pupils in her class.

Around 25% of French pupils repeat a year (**redoubler**) at some point during their schooling because they have not reached the required standard. This is the case for Lucas, who is taking his *seconde* for the second time when we meet him at the beginning of the novel. The *seconde* is commonly retaken because the marks obtained at the end of this year determine which kind of qualification a student can study towards in their final two years at school.

French exams are marked out of 20. An average mark of 10 out of 20 is needed to pass the French **baccalaureate**, which is the exam most French pupils take at 18. Lou's average of 18 – **mes dix-huit de moyenne** – is extremely rare and easily makes her the best student in her class, if not the whole school (16 out of 20 in the French *bac* is equivalent to three A grades at A Level). Lucas, on the other hand, routinely receives marks of 2, 1 or even 0 and his average is 5.5.

State boarding schools (*internats*) are common in France. Children might go to boarding school if their school is too far away from home or not well-served by public transport. They might also want to specialise in a subject not offered at their local school. They live at school during the week and go home at weekends.

---

high school *le lycée* where French students go usually between the ages of 15 and 18. The first year is known as *seconde*, the second year is *première* and the final year is *terminale*. Lou and Lucas are in *seconde*

redoubler to repeat a school year a second (or third) time because it wasn't passed the first time round

baccalaureate *le baccalauréat (le bac)* exam taken at the end of secondary school, equivalent to British A Levels

---

Activité 3

Choisissez trois personnages du roman et pour chacun écrivez une phrase pour décrire leur scolarité en vous servant du vocabulaire de la vie scolaire française. Par exemple: La mère de No n'est pas allée au lycée. Elle a arrêté l'école au collège. Elle n'a pas eu le bac.

Tips for assessment

Learn the vocabulary of the French school system mentioned on page 26 and at the end of this chapter. You will need it to answer questions relating to education in the exam.

Homelessness in France

Like many European countries, France has a substantial homeless population. According to Monsieur Marin, 'selon les estimations il y a entre 200 000 et 300 000 personnes sans domicile fixe, 40% sont des femmes, le chiffre est en augmentation constante. Et parmi les SDF âgés de 16 à 18 ans, la proportion de femmes atteint 70%' *(p. 33)*.

Around half of France's *sans domicile fixe* population live in Paris or the **Île-de-France** region. In the mid-2000s, makeshift camps began springing up on the edges of the ring road (*périphérique*) which circles Paris. Lou sees these camps for the first time when she is coming back from her aunt's house.

> **Key quotation**
>
> [...] j'ai vu les campements de SDF sur les talus, sous les ponts, j'ai découvert les tentes, les tôles, les baraquements, je n'avais jamais vu ça, je ne savais pas que ça existait, là, juste au bord, mon père et ma mère regardaient droit devant eux, [...].
> *(p. 178)*

Vigan uses Lou's surprise to remind us that most Parisians are unaware of the extent of the city's homelessness problem. Homeless people are invisible; they live on the edges of the city, where people like Lou's parents pass by without noticing them.

A homeless camp on the ring road in northern Paris

l'Île-de-France Paris and its surrounding area; people who live here are known as *Franciliens*

Tips for assessment

Learn the vocabulary for homelessness in France (see page 31). You will need it to discuss No's situation in the exam.

It is estimated that around 500 homeless people die on the streets of Paris every year. In the mid-2000s, social justice activists began publicising these numbers in the hope of convincing the French government to spend more on getting homeless people off the streets and into proper accommodation. In the novel, Vigan uses the story of Mouloud to remind the reader of this shocking situation.

Activité 4

Relisez la description de la mort de Mouloud (pp. 80–81). Imaginez que vous êtes un(e) journaliste du journal quotidien français *Le Monde*. Rédigez un article de 200–250 mots racontant la mort de Mouloud et les réactions des gens du quartier.

Comment s'en sortir?

The question of who can help the homeless is explored throughout the novel. In France, some state-funded aid is available for homeless people. In January, No is given a bed in a *centre d'hébergement d'urgence* for two weeks. But her days are made no easier by this relative stability.

> **Key quotation**
>
> **À huit heures trente, chaque matin, elle est dehors. Dehors pour toute une journée. Il faut tuer le temps. Marcher pour ne pas avoir froid. Trouver un endroit abrité pour s'asseoir. Il faut traverser tout Paris pour un repas chaud. Prendre un ticket. Attendre. Repartir. Demander de l'argent à la sortie d'un magasin ou dans le métro. Quand elle a la force.** *(p. 101)*

It is almost impossible for homeless people to find work: **'Pas d'adresse, pas de boulot'** *(p. 101)*. Although France has a minimum wage (*le SMIC*), low-paid workers like No are often paid below this level. They are paid wholly or partly in cash (*au noir*) so that their employer does not need to meet legal requirements.

Various kinds of support are in place for people like No. She has been assigned a social worker (*une assistante sociale*) but it is up to her to arrange and then keep her appointments. The social worker is powerless to help her if No does not take responsibility for attending: **'elle ne peut pas faire grand-chose si No ne vient plus'** *(p. 185)*.

The social worker helps her apply for benefits and finds her a place in a **day centre** where she can get help applying for work: 'un centre d'accueil de jour qui s'occupe de réinsertion pour jeunes femmes en grande difficulté' (*p. 130*). This is different to the **emergency shelter** where No stays for two weeks before she goes to Lou's flat.

The final centre where Lou's father seems to have secured No a place is a more permanent **reintegration shelter** aimed at helping the homeless move back into a conventional life of work and a home.

When No vanishes, Lou's father gets back in touch with the *assistante sociale*. According to her, people who live on the streets are hard to help.

> **Key quotation**
>
> Elle n'avait plus aucune nouvelle, elle a dit c'est souvent comme ça, vous savez, les gens de la rue ne sont pas fiables, ils repartent comme ils sont venus.
> (*p. 196*)

day centre *le centre d'accueil de jour* a place where homeless people can go to use the computers and look for work

emergency shelter *le centre d'hébergement d'urgence* a state-funded centre which provides short-term accommodation – dormitories and showers – for homeless people

reintegration shelter *le centre d'hébergement et de réinsertion sociale* a state-funded centre where a person in great need of help can live while trying to find a job and complete administrative procedures

This raises some interesting questions in the novel:

- Are people homeless because they are hard to help or because they do not want to accept the help they are given?
- Are homeless people given the help they really need?
- Lou and her parents give No food, clothes and a safe place to wash and sleep, but this does not seem to solve all No's problems. What other kinds of help does No need?

Vigan does not give any answers to these questions in the novel: she presents the reader with a set of circumstances and leaves us to draw our own conclusions.

No at the station, from the 2010 film adaptation

Writing about context

The context in which a novel is written and set influences how the author presents their story. Understanding the context enables you to understand the novel on a deeper level. However, be careful not to make sweeping statements which may go beyond the author's intention. For example, while it is important to understand how the context of homelessness in France relates to No's story, in an exam you should avoid writing about homelessness in general. Make sure you use your background knowledge to make points about the novel and about No's particular situation.

Vocabulary

l'assistant(e) social(e) social worker

l'association (f) (caritative) charity

le centre d'accueil de jour day centre

le centre d'hébergement d'urgence emergency shelter

le centre d'hébergement et de réinsertion sociale reintegration shelter

la CMU (Couverture Maladie Universelle) state benefit which reimburses medical costs

la copie piece of written work handed in as homework or completed in class

le devoir homework

les devoirs (m) collective noun for homework

l'exposé (m) oral presentation

l'internat (m) boarding school

la note mark which indicates the level of a piece of schoolwork; in France marks are given out of 20

le quartier neighbourhood, district

la récréation (la récré) break between two classes

la rentrée start of the new school year

le renvoi short-term suspension of a pupil

les restos du cœur charity which provides hot food

le SAMU social group of French homeless charities

le / la sans-abri person without a fixed address

la scolarité schooling, education

le / la SDF (sans domicile fixe) person without a fixed address

le SMIC (salaire minimum de croissance) minimum wage

Useful phrases

Pour mieux apprécier le roman... In order to better appreciate the novel...

En faisant référence aux événements réels... By referring to real events...

Une impression de vraisemblance est créée en... A sense of realism is created by...

Vigan combine la réalité et la fiction afin de... Vigan combines reality with fiction in order to...

Il y a un rapport entre... et... There is a connection between... and...

Vigan s'inspire de l'actualité parisienne pour... Vigan is inspired by current events in Paris to...

L'intrigue nous aide à comprendre la situation des SDF The plot helps us to understand homeless people's situation

Vigan nous présente le problème sans le commenter Vigan presents us with the problem without commenting on it

Vigan fait référence à des endroits réels Vigan refers to real places

Characters

Main characters

Lou Bertignac

Lou Bertignac is the novel's narrator and as the main protagonist, the character we know best. When we meet her she is 13 years old and lives in a flat in Paris with her parents. Her classmates refer to her as 'the brain' (*le cerveau*) because she is intellectually advanced for her age. She has an IQ of 160 and has consequently skipped two years of school. But she is socially awkward, clumsy and physically immature. She is the youngest in her class and feels out of place among 15- and 16-year-olds like Axelle Vernoux and Léa Germain. Lou is very shy and absolutely hates public speaking but she has an eloquent and expressive **interior monologue**.

> **Key quotations**
>
> J'ai horreur des exposés, j'ai horreur de prendre la parole devant la classe [...].
> *(p. 11)*
>
> [...] je regarde mes pieds, mon lacet est défait, comme d'habitude. D'où vient qu'avec un Q.I. de 160 je ne suis pas foutue de faire un lacet?
> *(p. 13)*
>
> [...] j'évite les récits et les discours, je me contente de répondre aux questions que l'on me pose, je garde pour moi l'excédent, l'abondance, ces mots que je multiplie en silence pour approcher la vérité.
> *(pp. 28–29)*

interior monologue *le monologue intérieur* a speech carried out by one person inside their head

Lou sees herself as different from those around her. She describes herself as an outsider and a misfit.

> **Key quotation**
>
> [...] dans ma nouvelle classe les élèves m'appellent le cerveau, ils m'ignorent ou me fuient, comme si j'avais une maladie contagieuse, mais au fond je sais que c'est moi qui n'arrive pas à leur parler, à rire avec eux, je me tiens à l'écart.
> *(p. 29)*

Activité 1

> Depuis toute la vie je me suis toujours sentie en dehors, où que je sois, en dehors de l'image, de la conversation, en décalage, comme si j'étais seule à entendre des bruits ou des paroles que les autres ne perçoivent pas, et sourde aux mots qu'ils semblent entendre, comme si j'étais hors du cadre, de l'autre côté d'une vitre immense et invisible.
> *(p. 19)*

a) Traduisez cette description de Lou en anglais.

b) Écrivez un paragraphe de 150 mots pour dire si vous êtes d'accord avec cette opinion qu'a Lou de son propre caractère.

When Lou is eight, her teachers notice that she is *renfermée* and *solitaire*. She demonstrates a *maturité inquiétante* and is described by her psychologist as *une enfant intellectuellement précoce*. After the death of Thaïs, Lou becomes less close to her parents. She spends four years away at boarding school and when she finally returns home, she spends a lot of time on her own or neglected by her mother.

Activité 2

Lisez l'histoire de la chute de vélo *(pp. 212–213)*. Imaginez que vous êtes la dame sur le banc. Écrivez une description de la scène en 100 mots. Que voyez-vous? Que faites-vous? Que pensez-vous?

Lou understands that she is different from other people: **'Parfois il me semble qu'à l'intérieur de moi quelque chose fait défaut, un fil inversé, une pièce défectueuse'** *(p. 77)*. Lou's use of mechanical vocabulary here shows that she thinks of herself as a machine which has gone wrong. She sees her difference in negative terms, like a construction error or a missing part: **'une erreur de fabrication, non pas quelque chose en plus, comme on pourrait le croire, mais quelque chose qui manque'** *(p. 77)*.

In the first part of the novel, Lou is often sad and lonely; she avoids spending time with her parents and hangs around outside after school rather than going straight home: **'certains soirs je n'ai pas envie de rentrer chez moi, à cause de toute cette tristesse qui colle aux murs, à cause du vide dans les yeux de ma mère'** *(p. 99)*.

Lou's solitary hobbies include looking up new words, checking facts in encyclopaedias and conducting experiments on household objects.

Lou's extreme intelligence is shown by the way she tries to use science to understand life. When she starts thinking about kissing Lucas, she focuses on the logistics of kissing rather than the way it might make her feel: **'Quand on embrasse, dans quel sens faut-il tourner la langue? (La logique voudrait que ce soit dans le sens des aiguilles d'une montre […])'** *(p. 79)*.

The moment when she asks No if she knows the answer to this question is one of the happiest moments in the novel. No laughs until she cries, and her answer demonstrates the extent to which Lou's view of the world differs from that of those around her: **'– T'as de ces questions! Y a pas de sens pour embrasser, on n'est pas des machines à laver!'** *(p. 105)*.

On Sundays, Lou conducts scientific experiments on household objects. Lou describes her friendship with No as if it were a similar kind of experiment: **'c'est une sorte d'expérience aussi, de très haut niveau, une expérience de grande envergure menée contre le destin'** *(p. 151)*.

When No comes to live with her, Lou finally has a friend. She loves spending time with No, involving her in the family routine and talking to her about her life at school. The presence of No also helps Lou overcome her shyness with Lucas. Thanks to No, Lou feels able to spend time at Lucas's flat after school. Lucas's flat is a sanctuary for Lou. She feels safe when she is with Lucas and No. Both of them protect her because she is so much younger than they are: **'je me glisse entre No et lui [Lucas], je sens la chaleur de leurs corps contre le mien et il me semble que plus rien jamais ne pourra nous arriver'** *(p. 139)*.

It is Lou's need for companionship, coupled with her strong sense of social justice, which drives Lou to keep on helping No until No abandons her.

Key quotation

[…] hier j'étais là, avec elle, on aurait pu j'en suis sûre dessiner un cercle autour de nous, un cercle dont je n'étais pas exclue, un cercle qui nous enveloppait, et qui, pour quelques minutes, nous protégeait du monde. *(p. 19)*

Lou et No, from the 2010 film adaptation

Lou is constantly comparing herself to other people. But her high IQ means that she does not behave like other people. As her psychologist explains: **'les intellectuellement précoces ont une grande capacité à conceptualiser, à appréhender le monde, mais [...] ils peuvent être démunis face à des situations relativement simples'** *(p. 111).*

Key quotation

Je voudrais seulement être comme les autres, j'envie leur aisance, leurs rires, leurs histoires, je suis sûre qu'ils possèdent quelque chose que je n'ai pas, j'ai longtemps cherché dans le dictionnaire un mot qui dirait la facilité, l'insouciance, la confiance et tout, un mot que je collerais dans mon cahier, en lettres capitales, comme une incantation.
(pp. 53–54)

Lou's inability to deal with everyday situations is demonstrated throughout the novel. Lou has been brought up in a white, middle-class household and unlike No and Lucas she is very **naive** and not at all streetwise. She has learnt a huge amount about science, art and literature from books, but she knows almost nothing about life. This naivety is demonstrated at several points in the narrative, for example, in the scene where Lou first meets No's homeless friends in Section 3 *(p. 58).* When Roger offers everyone except Momo a slice of his *saucisson sec*, Lou assumes that Momo is not included because he does not have enough teeth to chew the meat properly. The reader, on the other hand, understands that Momo's name is short for Mohamed, and that this Muslim name indicates that Momo does not eat pork. Vigan uses moments like this to remind us that despite her articulate prose and her high IQ, Lou is still a child.

Similarly, after No starts working at the hotel, Lou describes how No changes without being able to explain what is causing these changes: 'maintenant je sais qu'il lui est arrivé quelque chose, quelque chose qu'on ne peut pas dire, quelque chose qui fait basculer' *(p. 175).*

Key quotation

Depuis qu'elle travaille de nuit No n'est plus la même, c'est quelque chose à l'intérieur d'elle, comme une immense fatigue ou un insondable dégoût, quelque chose qui nous échappe.
(p. 197)

---

naive *naïf / naïve* showing a lack of experience, wisdom or judgement; childlike or innocent

As with the example regarding Momo, Vigan leaves enough evidence in the text for the reader to work out what kind of work No is doing without Lou realising it herself.

The moment when Lou runs away with No marks her shift from childhood to adulthood. Lou glimpses No's world and then learns how it feels to be abandoned by someone she trusts. As she walks home across Paris, Lou realises that she has changed: 'Quelque chose venait de m'arriver. Quelque chose dont je devais comprendre le sens, dont je devais prendre la mesure, pour toute la vie' *(p. 244)*.

Lou has a strong sense of justice. She often feels that she is the only one who cares about changing the unfair society in which she lives. It is this belief in social justice, coupled with her determination, which leads her to try and make a difference to No. Monsieur Marin describes her as a **utopian** (*une utopiste*) *(p. 165)* for believing that she can change the world. When No is forced to leave Lou's home, Lou realises that life is more complicated than she thought.

> **Key quotation**
>
> La vérité c'est que je n'arrive pas à faire mes lacets et que je suis équipée de fonctionnalités merdiques qui ne servent à rien.
> *(p. 191)*

But despite a series of setbacks, she continues to fight for No until No prevents her from doing so by leaving her. Lou even leaves home with the intention of accompanying No to Ireland.

Despite her young age, Lou hates being spoken to like a child and listening to her mother and No makes her jealous: 'j'avoue que ça me pique à l'intérieur, comme des petites aiguilles qu'on enfoncerait dans mon cœur' *(p. 150)*. Vigan uses the relationship between No and Lou's mother to remind the reader that for all Lou's intelligence, Lou is much younger than No. Lou's mother treats No like a grown-up and her language reflects this: 'À dix-huit ans on est adulte, ça se sent à la manière dont les gens s'adressent à vous, avec une forme d'égard, de distance, pas comme on s'adresse à un enfant' *(p. 150)*.

Activité 3

Mettez-vous à la place de Lou. Écrivez une lettre de 100 à 150 mots à vos parents pour expliquer pourquoi vous avez décidé de partir en Irlande avec No.

utopian *l'utopiste (m / f)* an idealist, a dreamer

No (Nolwenn)

No is a homeless young woman of 18 whom Lou meets at the gare d'Austerlitz. When she turned 18, No lost her place in care and found herself on the streets of Paris. When Lou meets her she is living rough. Sometimes she sleeps at friends' houses, sometimes at homeless shelters, sometimes on the streets: **'elle vit dans la rue mais elle n'aime pas qu'on le dise'** *(p. 58)*.

No can be distrustful and aggressive. She will talk about life on the streets but she is reluctant to share details of her family. Eventually she tells Lou that she was taken into a foster home when she was 12. Her mother lives in Ivry, a working-class suburb to the south-east of Paris, and does not want anything to do with No. No is the first person whom Lou feels she can talk to about herself. Unlike her classmates, No does not care about outward appearances and branded clothing: she does not judge Lou for being different and she loves listening to Lou talk.

> **Key quotations**
>
> [...] il suffisait de voir son regard, comme il était vide, pour savoir qu'elle n'avait personne pour l'attendre, pas de maison, pas d'ordinateur, et peut-être nulle part où aller.
> *(p. 19)*
>
> Elle n'aime pas les adultes, elle ne fait pas confiance. Elle boit de la bière, se ronge les ongles, traîne derrière elle une valise à roulettes qui contient toute sa vie, elle fume les cigarettes qu'on lui donne, du tabac roulé quand elle peut en acheter, ferme les yeux pour s'extraire du monde.
> *(p. 59)*

Lou's descriptions of No emphasise how worn-out No appears. No seems physically exhausted but she also looks world-weary. She is still a teenager, but she already has the life-experience of a much older person.

> **Key quotations**
>
> Elle avait l'air si jeune. En même temps, il m'avait semblé qu'elle connaissait vraiment la vie, ou plutôt qu'elle connaissait de la vie quelque chose qui faisait peur.
> *(p. 20)*
>
> [...] elle a l'air si fatiguée, pas seulement à cause des cernes sous ses yeux, ni de ses cheveux emmêlés, retenus par un vieux chouchou, ni ses vêtements défraîchis, il y a ce mot qui me vient à l'esprit, *abîmée*, ce mot qui fait mal, [...].
> *(pp. 26–27)*

As well as being aggressive and distrustful, No is also proud. She refuses to take any of Lou's belongings and she would rather manage on her own than be helped by Lou. No is too concerned with her own situation to realise that Lou needs her at least as much as she needs Lou. As Lou says: **'je voudrais lui dire qu'elle me manque, même si c'est absurde, même si c'est elle qui manque de tout, de tout ce qu'il faut pour vivre, mais moi aussi je suis toute seule et je suis venue la chercher'** *(p. 93)*.

When Lou sees No at the *soupe populaire de la rue Clément* she is shocked by how much No has changed in the three weeks since they last saw each other: **'comme elle a changé, cette amertume à ses lèvres, cet air de défaite, d'abandon'** *(p. 91)*.

People queue outside a soup kitchen in Paris

Once No becomes settled with Lou's family she begins to confide in them. But it is Lou's mother she talks to, rather than Lou herself. This annoys Lou who feels left out and rejected by her mother.

Activité 4

Utilisez la liste d'adjectifs ci-dessous pour écrire des phrases sur la vie de No. Attention aux accords! Par exemple: La vie à la rue est dangereuse. No se sent protégée chez Lou.

sale	fatigué	violent
dangereux	affamé	exploité
courageux	têtu	pauvre
abandonné	protégé	

No's story is a harrowing one. Her mother, Suzanne, lived in rural Normandy. She became pregnant with No after she was gang-raped in a barn at the age of 15. Suzanne never got over the trauma of her daughter's conception and refused to have anything to do with No. Until she was seven, No was brought up by her grandparents. When her grandmother died, she went to live with her mother and her boyfriend in Choisy-le-Roi, a suburb to the south-east of Paris.

When the boyfriend, whom No refers to as *l'homme à la moto*, left them, No's mother started to drink and become violent towards her daughter. Eventually, social services arranged for No to be taken away from her mother. When she was 12 she was placed in a foster family.

Key quotation

Monsieur et Madame Langlois lui achetaient les vêtements dont elle avait besoin, lui donnaient de l'argent de poche, s'inquiétaient de ses mauvais résultats scolaires.
(p. 149)

No is sent to an *internat éducatif* when she begins running away from her foster family. Here she meets Loïc and Geneviève. After Loïc and Geneviève leave school, No's behaviour deteriorates. She is eventually placed in care until her 18th birthday.

Like her mother, No left school without any qualifications. This makes it extremely difficult for her to find a job: **'Elle a arrêté l'école en troisième, elle ne parle aucune langue étrangère, ne sais pas utiliser un ordinateur, elle n'a jamais travaillé'** *(p. 139)*.

Despite her lack of qualifications and experience, No eventually finds a job: **'Tous les matins, à partir de sept heures, No est femme de chambre dans un hôtel près de Bastille'** *(p. 141)*.

No is exploited by her boss. He does not pay her for all the overtime she works and she is not allowed proper breaks.

After No has been working for a few weeks, Lou notices that she is increasingly unhappy. No is reluctant to confide in Lou and resists Lou's attempts to help her: **'– Je suis pas de ta famille, Lou. C'est ça qu'il faut que tu comprennes, je serai jamais de ta famille'** *(p. 174)*.

No's only family is her mother who refuses to have anything to do with her. Despite knowing how her mother feels, No decides to go to Ivry with Lou to see her. When the girls arrive at the flat, her mother refuses even to acknowledge their presence. No is deeply hurt by her mother's rejection of her. Her drinking increases after this incident.

Just before Lou goes on holiday with her parents for a few days, she notices that No is stealing pills from her parents' medicine cabinet. While they are away, something happens to No. She stops answering their calls and when they return they find empty drink bottles and pill packets in her room. No comes back in the early hours of the morning. She misses her appointment with her social worker and spends most of her time locked in the bathroom or crying in her bedroom. She will not confide in Lou and so the reader can only guess what is happening at work. All we know from Lou is that No is now working night shifts and that her behaviour changed when she started working nights.

No's lonely and abusive childhood has made her emotionally insecure. Lou notes that No often asks her the same two questions. Lou's comment on the second question is a way for Vigan to anticipate the story's denouement.

> **Key quotations**
>
> – On est ensemble, hein, Lou, on est ensemble?
>
> Il y a une autre question qui revient souvent, et comme à la première je réponds oui, elle veut savoir si je lui fais confiance, si j'ai confiance en elle.
>
> Je ne peux pas m'empêcher de penser à cette phrase que j'ai lue quelque part, je ne sais plus où: celui qui s'assure sans cesse de ta confiance sera le premier à la trahir.
> *(p. 134)*

When Lucas finds several 50-euro notes in No's pocket, he loses his temper with her. Even though Lou never spells out how No is getting so much money, even she has realised that No is getting paid for sex: **'elle le regarde et ça veut dire qu'est-ce que tu crois, […] comment tu crois qu'on peut sortir de cette merde'** *(p. 227)*.

When No is forced to leave Lucas's flat, she lets Lou think they are going to Ireland. But instead she vanishes once more, abandoning Lou in the waiting room at the *gare St-Lazare*.

> **Activité 5**
>
> Imaginez que vous êtes No. Écrivez une lettre de 70 à 80 mots à Lou pour lui expliquer pourquoi vous l'avez laissée à la gare.

Lucas Muller

Lucas Muller is a 17-year-old boy in Lou's class. Lou first mentions Lucas in the opening section of the novel, when she is describing how embarrassed she feels when her teacher, Monsieur Marin, asks her about the topic of her presentation (*exposé*). Lucas's smile makes Lou feel brave enough to speak in front of the whole class.

> **Key quotation**
>
> Lucas me sourit. Ses yeux sont immenses, je pourrais me noyer à l'intérieur, disparaître, ou laisser le silence engloutir Monsieur Marin et toute la classe avec lui.
> *(p. 12)*

Lucas in the street with Lou and No, from the 2010 film adaptation

---

Key quotation

C'est un garçon particulier. Je le sais depuis le début. Pas seulement à cause de son air en colère, son dédain ou sa démarche de voyou. À cause de son sourire, un sourire d'enfant.
(p. 38)

Unlike her other classmates, such as Léa Germain and Axelle Vernoux, Lucas is nice to Lou. He smiles at her in class, talks to her at break and invites her back to his place just before Christmas. Lucas affectionately calls Lou 'Pépite'. Lucas is two years older than the other pupils in the class because he has failed the year twice and has had to repeat it. He lives on his own: his father left suddenly for Brazil when he was 15, and his mother has recently moved in with her new boyfriend in Neuilly, a rich suburb to the west of Paris. At school, Lucas is disruptive and sullen. He never takes notes in class and frequently gets 0 out of 20 for his homework.

Key quotations

Je lui parle de Lucas, de ses dix-sept ans, de son corps qui semble si lourd, si dense, et cette façon qu'il a de me regarder, comme si j'étais une fourmi égarée, ses copies blanches et l'excellence de mes notes, ses trois jours de renvoi et mes devoirs cités en exemple, sa douceur avec moi, pourtant à l'extrême opposé de lui.
(p. 104)

J'aime être à côté de lui, respirer son odeur, effleurer son bras. Je pourrais passer des heures comme ça, à le regarder, son nez droit, ses mains, sa mèche qui retombe devant ses yeux.
(p. 145)

Activité 6

a) Faites une liste de six adjectifs qui décrivent Lucas: par exemple 'paresseux' (lazy).

b) Dans un dictionnaire, cherchez le contraire de chaque adjectif: par exemple, le contraire de 'paresseux' est 'travailleur' ou 'actif'.

c) Mettez les 12 adjectifs que vous avez trouvés au féminin: par exemple, 'paresseux' devient 'paresseuse', 'actif' devient 'active'.

d) Soulignez tous les adjectifs au féminin qui décrivent Lou. À votre avis, Lou est-elle le contraire de Lucas? Justifiez votre réponse dans une phrase de 30 à 40 mots.

Lou tells No that she is the opposite of Lucas but they in fact have a lot in common. Both are neglected by their mothers and both feel out of place at school. Both think that the world is unfair and both care about No and want to help her. When No is living with Lou's family, Lucas gives Lou comics, chocolate and cigarettes for her. No is a shared secret which brings Lou and Lucas closer together. **'Nous avons notre secret'** *(p. 122)*. When No leaves Lou's flat and begins to live at Lucas's place, Lou and Lucas become even more complicit through the shared task of taking care of No: **'Au lycée nous parlons d'elle à voix basse, nous avons des codes pour évaluer l'état de la situation, des sourires complices et des airs entendus'** *(p. 199)*.

> **Key quotation**
>
> **Il est le roi, l'insolent, le rebelle, je suis la première de la classe, docile et silencieuse. Il est le plus âgé et je suis la plus jeune, il est le plus grand et je suis minuscule.**
> *(p. 122)*

As well as helping No, the friendship between Lou and Lucas is beneficial to both of them. Lucas helps Lou to feel both more confident and more mature. Her classmates are nicer to her when they see how much Lucas likes her. Lou seems to be a good influence on Lucas in the classroom. As Monsieur Marin rather sarcastically puts it: **'tiens, Monsieur Muller, vous voilà en utile compagnie, Mademoiselle Bertignac pourra éventuellement vous transmettre un peu de son sérieux'** *(p. 121)*. Lucas is much more creative than Lou: he plays the guitar, loves making up stories, and is particularly good at mimicking his classmates and teachers. Lucas is four years older than Lou and much more worldly-wise. He introduces her to bands and television shows, smokes, and flirts with Axelle and Léa. He also understands aspects of No's life which Lou is too sheltered and naive to notice.

> **Key quotation**
>
> Ce que j'aime chez Lucas c'est qu'il est capable d'imaginer les histoires les plus invraisemblables et d'en parler pendant des heures, avec plein de détails, comme si cela suffisait pour qu'elles adviennent, […].
> *(p. 164)*

Because the story is **narrated** by Lou, we never hear Lucas's thoughts. But his violent reaction to the 50-euro notes which he finds in No's pocket suggests to us, although perhaps not to Lou herself, that he is angry and worried because No is selling her body for money. Lucas's anger demonstrates that he feels both responsible for No and powerless to help her. It marks the point in the story where Lou and Lucas stop being able to protect No. At the end of the novel Lucas, who is moving to Neuilly to live with his mother, finally kisses Lou. It is not clear whether this is the end of their relationship or the beginning of a new stage in it.

narrate *raconter* to tell in a story-like format

Activité 7

Relisez l'épisode où Lou emmène No chez Lucas *(pp. 112–113)*. Imaginez que vous êtes Lucas. Écrivez une description de 80 à 100 mots de vos pensées quand vous voyez No chez vous pour la première fois. Quelles sont vos réactions, vos impressions et vos inquiétudes?

Upgrade

Make a list of 20 adjectives to describe the three main characters and learn them, as they will help you to prepare for character questions in the exam.
Some adjectives could apply to more than one character; you could use a table like this to record them:

Lou	No	Lucas
timide	assurée	assuré

Minor characters

Le père de Lou (Bernard Bertignac)

Lou's father works in an unspecified office job and runs the household. He cooks for
Lou every night and looks after her and her mother. He is a stable and reassuring,
though rather distant, presence in the novel.

> **Key quotation**
>
> [...] **je vois bien qu'il est triste, il fait des efforts pour paraître enjoué,
> mais sa voix sonne faux.**
> *(p. 42)*
>
> **Il ne s'énerve jamais, il a une veste en cuir, une épouse malade dont il
> s'occupe très bien et une fille adolescente un peu pénible, [...].**
> *(p. 95)*

Lou and her father, from the 2010 film adaptation

La mère de Lou (Anouk Bertignac)

At the beginning of the narrative, Lou's mother is characterised by her absence.
Although she lives with Lou and her father she is rarely present: she has depression
and is often asleep. She rarely eats with the family and spends hours on the sofa
staring into space. When Lou comes home from school, her mother sometimes
performs the gestures of a caring mother but her actions are mechanical.

Quand je rentre chez moi je la trouve assise sur son fauteuil, au milieu du salon. Elle n'allume pas la lumière, du matin jusqu'au soir elle reste là, je le sais, sans bouger, elle déplie une couverture sur ses genoux, elle attend que le temps passe. Quand j'arrive elle se lève, accomplit une succession de gestes et de déplacements, par habitude ou par automatisme, sort du placard les paquets de biscuits, pose les verres sur la table, s'assoit près de moi sans rien dire, ramasse la vaisselle, range ce qui reste, passe un coup d'éponge.

(p.54)

Activité 9

En français, une des fonctions de l'imparfait est de montrer qu'un événement se déroulait de façon habituelle au passé. Relisez l'extrait ci-dessus. Réécrivez la description des actions de la mère de Lou en mettant à l'imparfait les verbes au présent. Par exemple: Quand je rentrais chez moi je la trouvais assise sur son fauteuil…

Lou uses imagery borrowed from the world of the theatre to suggest that she and her mother do not have any real connection: 'nous sommes dans un jeu de rôle, elle est la mère et moi la fille, chacune respecte son texte et suit les indications' *(p. 55)*.

On the night when Lou asks her parents if No can come and stay, her mother astonishes both her and her father by agreeing to meet No. This moment marks the start of Lou's mother's recovery. By helping No she regains her own sense of purpose.

[…] ma mère est restée avec nous jusqu'à la fin du repas. Pour la première fois depuis longtemps il m'a semblé qu'elle était vraiment là, que sa présence n'était pas une simple figuration, elle était là tout entière.
(p. 115)

No's presence in Lou's family seems to energise Lou's mother. She spends a lot of time with No and is the person No feels best able to confide in: 'c'est ma mère qui arrive le mieux à la faire parler' *(p. 130)*.

> Ma mère a recommencé à feuilleter des magazines, elle a emprunté des livres à la bibliothèque, visité une ou deux expositions. Elle s'habille, se coiffe, se maquille, dîne avec nous tous les soirs, [...].
> *(pp. 134–135.)*

No's presence also encourages her mother to tell stories about Lou's childhood. This reveals that Thaïs's death did not rob her of all her memories: **'J'écoutais et je me disais c'est incroyable, ma mère a des souvenirs. Ainsi, tout n'a pas été effacé. Ma mère abrite dans sa mémoire des images en couleur, des images d'avant'** *(p. 157).*

Thaïs

Thaïs is Lou's baby sister. She was born when Lou was eight and died shortly afterwards. Lou's inability to talk about her own feelings means that she never tells us how she felt about her sister or her untimely death. But the detail with which she describes Thaïs and the care she takes when feeding and bathing her suggests that she loved her sister and was devastated by her death.

> Thaïs avait une bouche, un nez, des mains, des pieds, des doigts, des ongles. Thaïs ouvrait et fermait les yeux, bâillait, tétait, agitait ses petits bras, et cette mécanique de haute précision avait été fabriquée par mes parents.
> *(p. 46)*

Monsieur Marin

Monsieur Marin is Lou's form tutor and he also teaches SES (*Sciences économiques et sociales*). According to Lou, SES is **'Un cours où on étudie pas mal de trucs, par exemple la situation économique en France, la bourse, la croissance, les classes sociales, le quart-monde, et tout...'** *(p. 40).*

Lou describes Monsieur Marin as **'la Terreur du lycée'** *(p. 32)* because he is extremely strict.

> Il voit tout, entend tout, rien ne lui échappe.
> *(p. 33)*
>
> Tout le monde respecte Monsieur Marin.
> *(p. 33)*

Activité 10

Relisez la description des règles de la classe de Monsieur Marin dans la première section du roman *(p. 32)*. Écrivez une liste de ces règles en les mettant à la première personne. Par exemple: 'Il faut dire oui monsieur' → Je dois dire oui monsieur.

Lou seems to remind Monsieur Marin of himself at the same age. He describes Lou as an **'utopiste'** *(p. 165)*. At the end of his last class, he gives Lou a book: '**– C'est un livre qui a été très important pour moi quand j'étais jeune homme'** *(p. 249)*. As Lou leaves the classroom he simply says: '**– Ne renoncez pas'** *(p. 249)*.

Axelle Vernoux and Léa Germain

Lou almost always refers to these two classmates as a pair. They epitomise the fashionable and sophisticated adolescent girls who populate Lou's *lycée*. Before the novel's action begins they invite Lou to a party. Lou recounts this episode in Section 1 *(pp. 34–35)*. Lou was planning to attend but her nerve fails her at the last minute and she stays at home instead. This is why Axelle and Léa are not speaking to Lou at the beginning of the novel; they look down on her and laugh when she is put on the spot by Monsieur Marin.

> **Key quotation**
>
> **Axelle Vernoux et Léa Germain pouffent en silence derrière leurs mains, une dizaine de bracelets tintent de plaisir à leurs poignets.**
> *(p. 11)*

Activité 11

Imaginez que vous êtes Léa ou Axelle. Écrivez un paragraphe de 80 à 100 mots pour décrire Lou. À quoi ressemble-t-elle ? Que fait-elle en classe ? Pourquoi ne l'aimez-vous pas ?

Axelle and Léa are in awe of Lucas. They become much more respectful towards Lou as her friendship with Lucas develops.

Lucille, Corinne, Gauthier

Other members of Lou's class. She refers to them in passing *(p. 22)*.

Madame Cortanze

A psychologist whom Lou sees for a year after the sudden death of her baby sister *(pp. 49–50)*. She helps Lou to understand her difference from others by describing her as a high-performance racing car with highly complicated features *(p. 36)*. Lou uses this image throughout the novel. (See the 'Imagery' section in the chapter on Language, page 54.)

Roger and Momo

Homeless men whom No sometimes hangs out with at the *gare d'Austerlitz*. No is insistent that these are acquaintances rather than friends: **'dehors on n'a pas d'amis'** *(p. 58)*.

When No has started earning money, she walks past Momo without recognising him. When Lou points him out to her, she offers him a 20-euro note which Momo disdainfully refuses *(pp. 200–201)*.

Activité 12

Relisez l'épisode où Lou et No croisent Momo dans la rue *(pp. 200–201)*. Imaginez que vous êtes Momo. Écrivez un paragraphe de 80 à 100 mots pour expliquer vos actions. Pourquoi crachez-vous? Pourquoi n'acceptez-vous pas l'argent de No? À quoi pensez-vous en la voyant avec de l'argent?

La dame au kiosque

The lady who works in the newspaper kiosk at the *gare d'Austerlitz*. She sometimes gives No sweets and biscuits. When she sees Lou looking for No, she warns her about hanging out with No, suggesting they are from two very different worlds: **'Tu sais, mon p'tit, tu ne devrais pas traîner avec une fille comme ça. Moi, je l'aime bien, Nolwenn, mais c'est une fille de la rue, une fille qui vit dans un autre monde que le tien'** *(p. 74)*.

Tante Sylvie

Lou's father's sister. Whenever Aunt Sylvie spends time with Lou's family, she talks about Lou's mother Anouk as if she wasn't there. At Christmas Lou responds to Sylvie's remarks, defending her mother, and shocking the family into silence *(p. 84)*. Vigan includes this episode to demonstrate Lou's integrity and her fierce belief in fairness.

Mouloud

A homeless man who lived on the street near Lou's flat. He dies just before Christmas *(pp. 80–81)*.

> **Key quotation**
>
> **Depuis dix ans il vivait dehors, dans notre quartier. Il avait sa grille de métro, au croisement de deux rues, dans un renfoncement, juste à côté de la boulangerie. C'était son territoire.**
> *(p. 80)*

Mouloud refused to go into a homeless centre because they do not accept dogs. Vigan includes him in Lou's story to illustrate the plight of homeless people on the streets of Paris.

Geneviève

Geneviève went to the same school as No and No tells Lou that Geneviève sometimes used to let No stay with her. When Lou loses No after her *exposé*, she takes the metro to the *hypermarché* where Geneviève works to ask her about No *(pp. 86–87)*.

Loïc

Loïc is a boy whom No knew when she was at boarding school in Frénouville. No was in love with Loïc, and she tells Lou all about the fun they had together *(pp. 201–203)*. When he left school, Loïc went to work in Ireland. No tells Lou that he sent her dozens of letters. When she starts working, she saves money so that she can go to Ireland to find him.

> **Key quotation**
>
> **Les lettres de Loïc elle les a cachées quelque part, dans un endroit qu'elle seule connaît. Des dizaines de lettres.**
> *(p. 203)*

Activité 13

Relisez la description de Loïc *(pp. 225–226)*. Imaginez que vous êtes Loïc. Écrivez une lettre de 80 à 100 mots à No dans laquelle vous décrivez votre nouvelle vie en Irlande.

At the end of the novel, Geneviève tells Lou and Lucas that No has not heard from Loïc since he left school. She lied to Lou about the letters he sent her.

Activité 14

À votre avis, pourquoi No a-t-elle menti à Lou à propos de Loïc? Écrivez un paragraphe de 150 à 200 mots pour justifier votre opinion.

Madame Rivery

Lou's French teacher, whom she adores. Lucas knows that Madame Rivery is Lou's favourite teacher and behaves less disruptively in her classes as a result *(p. 107, p. 139)*.

La mère de No (Suzanne Pivet)

Suzanne lives on a housing estate in Ivry with her partner and their son *(pp. 131–133, pp. 146–148)*. She will not have anything to do with No and refuses to even open the door when No and Lou go to see her *(pp. 166–169)*.

Writing about characters

Be precise and as detailed as possible when you discuss the characters of the story. Make sure you know how to spell their names correctly. It can be useful to keep a file on the basic details the novel tells us about each of the characters, for example:

Full name of character	Age	Job	Appearance	Personality	Relationship to Lou
Anouk Bertignac	late 40s–early 50s	on long-term sick leave	tired, pale, no make-up	happy pre-Thaïs; depressed at the moment	mother

Vocabulary

enjoué(e) cheerful, happy

le geste gesture, movement

le jeu de rôle role play

manquer (à quelqu'un) to miss (someone)

manquer (quelque chose) to lack (something)

particulier(-ière) distinctive, unusual

le personnage mineur minor character

le personnage principal main character

le regard expression, gaze, look

renfermé(e) withdrawn

renoncer to give up

solitaire solitary, alone

se souvenir (de) to remember

se tenir à l'écart to shy away

Useful phrases

Il / Elle se comporte comme / comme si... He / She behaves like / as if…

Parfois il / elle... At times he / she…

Il / Elle se montre (in)capable de... He / She proves to be (in)capable of…

On peut le / la considérer... He / She can be considered…

Il / Elle veut avant tout... He / She wants more than anything…

On suppose que... We (pre)suppose that…

Ses réactions sont... His / Her reactions are…

On voit (souvent) qu'elles sont... We (often) see that they are…

Il y a des moments où... There are times when…

Character map

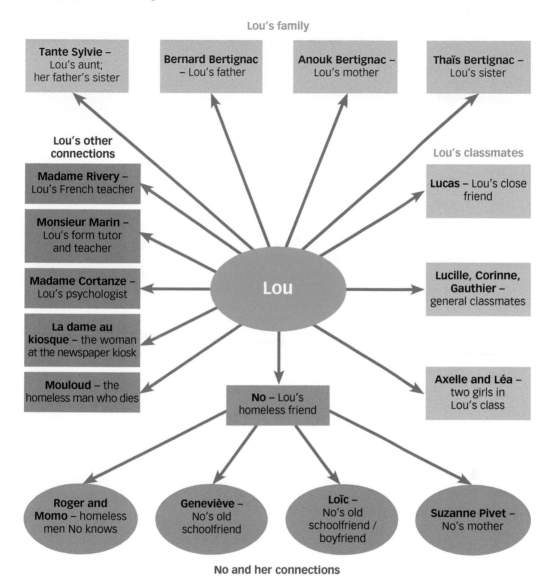

Lou's family

Tante Sylvie – Lou's aunt; her father's sister

Bernard Bertignac – Lou's father

Anouk Bertignac – Lou's mother

Thaïs Bertignac – Lou's sister

Lou's other connections

Madame Rivery – Lou's French teacher

Monsieur Marin – Lou's form tutor and teacher

Madame Cortanze – Lou's psychologist

La dame au kiosque – the woman at the newspaper kiosk

Mouloud – the homeless man who dies

Lou

Lou's classmates

Lucas – Lou's close friend

Lucille, Corinne, Gauthier – general classmates

Axelle and Léa – two girls in Lou's class

No – Lou's homeless friend

Roger and Momo – homeless men No knows

Geneviève – No's old schoolfriend

Loïc – No's old schoolfriend / boyfriend

Suzanne Pivet – No's mother

No and her connections

Lou's language

Because *No et moi* is a first-person narrative, all the words we read are Lou's. Lou hates speaking in class, but she is an eloquent and expressive writer. French is her favourite lesson at school and one of her hobbies is collecting new words.

> **Key quotation**
>
> [...] je cherche des nouveaux mots, c'est comme un vertige, parce qu'il y en a des milliers, je les découpe dans les journaux, pour les apprivoiser, je les colle sur les grands cahiers blancs [...].
> *(pp. 29–30)*

Vigan demonstrates Lou's knowledge through her linguistic choices. On p. 67, Lou borrows some words from 'Spleen', a well-known poem by the 19th-century French poet Charles Baudelaire: 'le ciel est bas et lourd comme dans les poésies'. (Baudelaire's original reads *Quand le ciel bas et lourd pèse comme un couvercle*.) This reference to a famous French poem demonstrates Lou's love of French language and literature. This passion for the French language is also demonstrated in the way Lou writes. She uses poetic features such as **repetition** and **imagery** to make her prose more elegant.

Repetition

Throughout the novel, Vigan uses the stylistic device of repetition to add emphasis and rhythm to Lou's prose. In the first extract below, Lou repeats the phrase *plus jamais* to emphasise how lonely her mother's depression makes Lou feel. In the second extract, Lou repeats *il suffit de* to highlight Lou's realisation that it is common to find mentally unstable people in the Paris metro.

> **Key quotations**
>
> Plus jamais elle ne pose la main sur moi, plus jamais elle ne touche mes cheveux, ne caresse ma joue, plus jamais elle ne me prend par le cou ou par la taille, plus jamais elle ne me serre contre elle.
> *(p. 55)*
>
> Il suffisait de regarder autour de soi. Il suffisait de voir le regard des gens, de compter ceux qui parlent tout seuls ou qui déraillent, il suffisait de prendre le métro.
> *(p. 241)*

repetition *la répétition* the repeating of a word or phrase, often used to add emphasis

imagery *les images (fpl)* visually descriptive language which conveys ideas or emotions

The entrance to a metro station in Paris

Activité 1

Relisez le premier paragraphe de la Section 2 (*p. 44*) qui commence *Quand j'étais petite*. À votre avis, pourquoi Lou répète-t-elle *Quand j'étais petite* trois fois dans ce paragraphe? Quel est l'effet de cette répétition sur le lecteur? Que ressentez-vous en lisant ce paragraphe?

Trouvez d'autres exemples de répétition dans le livre. Faites-en une liste. À votre avis, à quoi servent ces répétitions? Écrivez un paragraphe de 100 mots pour expliquer votre opinion.

Activité 2

Relisez le dernier paragraphe de l'exposé de Lou.

 … Il y a cette ville invisible, au cœur même de la ville. Cette femme qui dort chaque nuit au même endroit, avec son duvet et ses sacs. À même le trottoir. Ces hommes sous les ponts, dans les gares, ces gens allongés sur des cartons ou recroquevillés sur un banc. Un jour, on commence à les voir. Dans la rue, dans le métro. Pas seulement ceux qui font la manche. Ceux qui se cachent. On repère leur démarche, leur veste déformée, leur pull troué. Un jour on s'attache à une silhouette, à une personne, on pose des questions, on essaie de trouver des raisons, des explications. Et puis on compte. Les autres, des milliers. Comme le symptôme de notre monde malade. *Les choses sont ce qu'elles sont.* Mais moi je crois qu'il faut garder les yeux grands ouverts. Pour commencer.
(*p. 70*)

a) Soulignez les exemples de répétition utilisés par Lou. Quel est l'effet de ces répétitions sur le lecteur?

b) Traduisez ce paragraphe en anglais. Quelles difficultés remarquez-vous?

Imagery

Lou loves collecting new words and her interior monologue is full of sophisticated imagery which reflects her love of the French language. One example of this is the way she uses the recurring image of a high-performance racing car to describe her feelings. She was introduced to this way of describing herself by her psychologist, Madame Cortanze, and she uses it to express both her difference from other people and the difficulties she has fitting in.

> **Key quotation**
>
> Imagine que tu es une voiture extrêmemement moderne, équipée d'un nombre d'options et de fonctionnalités plus important que la plupart des voitures, que tu es plus rapide, plus performante. C'est une grande chance. Mais ce n'est pas si facile.
> *(p. 36)*

Lou uses this image throughout her narrative to express the uncertainty she often feels about herself.

> **Key quotations**
>
> [...] je ne sais pas déchiffrer les panneaux, je ne maîtrise pas mon véhicule, je me trompe sans cesse de direction, et j'ai plus souvent l'impression d'être enfermée sur une piste d'autos tamponneuses que de rouler sur un circuit de compétition.
> *(p. 36)*
>
> Si seulement j'étais équipée d'une fonction refroidissement d'urgence, cela m'arrangerait un peu.
> *(p. 37)*

Lou and No, from the 2010 film adaptation

Activité 3

Trouvez d'autres références à une voiture haute performance dans le texte. Écrivez un paragraphe de 150 à 200 mots pour répondre à la question 'Les références sont-elles efficaces?'

De l'infiniment petit à l'infiniment grand

Lou often refers to herself as *petite*. In French *petit(e)* can mean either 'small' or 'young' and Lou uses it to mean both these things. She also uses it metaphorically to mean 'insignificant' or 'unimportant'. In contrast, Lucas is *grand*. He is much taller than Lou and four years older than her. Lou also uses *grand* metaphorically to mean 'important' or 'significant'. Vigan alerts us to the importance of these two words in Lou's view of the world when she refers to the book which Lou's father buys her: *De l'infiniment petit à l'infiniment grand (p. 75)*. This book is a reference to Lou's way of thinking about the world. By the end of the book Lou is still *petite*, but she has metaphorically grown into someone who is both important and significant: **'quelque chose venait de m'arriver qui m'avait fait grandir'** *(p. 244)*.

Scientific imagery

Lou rarely refers to her own emotional state. Instead she uses scientific imagery to express how she feels. When Monsieur Marin asks her about the topic of her *exposé*, she says: **'Si je pouvais m'enfoncer cent kilomètres sous terre, du côté de la lithosphère, cela m'arrangerait'** *(p. 11)*. Vigan uses these scientific references to highlight the gap between Lou's intellectual ability and her emotional immaturity. She is able to make detailed reference to scientific facts but she cannot express how she feels.

Activité 4

Trouvez des moments dans le livre où Lou emploie un vocabulaire scientifique. Quel est l'effet de ses choix linguistiques? Quels sentiments essaie-t-elle d'exprimer ainsi?

Thèse, Antithèse, Synthèse

Lou is a conscientious student and she pays particular attention in French. Her teacher, Madame Rivery, has taught her how to structure her essays using a standard French essay-writing structure: Thesis, Antithesis, Synthesis (*Thèse, Antithèse, Synthèse*) and Lou incorporates what she has learnt into her daily life. When she asks her parents if No can come and stay with them, she prepares her arguments by writing a plan as she would for an essay at school *(pp. 107–108)*.

Activité 5

Imaginez que vous voulez convaincre No d'aller voir son assistante sociale. Préparez un plan comme celui de Lou: utilisez sa structure (Introduction; Grand 1 (thèse); Grand 2 (antithèse); Grand 3 (synthèse); Conclusion.

Colloquial language

The elegance of Lou's prose makes it easy to forget that we are reading the words of a 13-year-old girl. To remind us of Lou's age, Vigan includes some **colloquial expressions** which are mainly used by young people. The most frequent of these is *et tout* which Lou often uses to finish her sentences. *Et tout* is an informal expression which evokes an unspecified list of things. It is not acceptable in formal written or spoken French because it suggests laziness or imprecision. As Lou explains: *'et tout* **c'est pour toutes les choses qu'on pourrait ajouter mais qu'on passe sous silence, par paresse, par manque de temps, ou bien parce que ça ne se dit pas'** *(p. 30)*.

The fact that Lou explains this phrase shows that she thinks carefully about her own use of language. When she uses *et tout* she does so deliberately, perhaps as a way of sounding more like the teenagers she wants to be like.

Activité 6

Trouvez des exemples de 'et tout' dans le roman. À votre avis, est-ce que la présence de cette expression aide le lecteur à mieux comprendre?

Register

Register is the level of formality used in communication. Adults use a more formal register than children. Written French uses a more formal register than spoken French and the differences between formal and informal registers are greater in French than they are in English. Some situations, such as a job interview or an oral presentation, require a more formal register than other situations, such as a social gathering or a conversation between close friends or relatives. We constantly adjust our register depending on the context of the conversation we are having.

colloquial expressions *le langage familier* informal words or phrases, more commonly used in spoken language

register *le registre linguistique* the level of formality used in communication

Tu / Vous

In French, *tu* is used in informal conversations and *vous* is used in more formal situations. *Vous* is also used to address more than one person, even when *tu* would be used in the singular.

Tu veux venir au cinéma? suggests that a friend is being invited to the cinema by another friend. *Vous voulez venir au cinéma?* suggests either that a group of friends are being invited to the cinema by another friend, or that an acquaintance or work colleague is being invited to the cinema by someone he or she does not know very well.

Here are some more rules for using *tu* and *vous*:

- Young children use *tu* to address everyone.
- Teenagers are expected to use *vous* to address adults in positions of responsibility. Conversely, when adults use *vous* to address teenagers, they are showing their respect for them by treating them like grown-ups.
- Children and close relatives are always addressed using *tu*.

The rules governing when *vous* and *tu* are used are complicated and it is possible to offend someone by addressing them in the wrong way. If in doubt, use *vous* to address all adults until invited to use *tu* instead.

The rules in Francophone countries can vary. In French-speaking Canada, for example, *tu* is used more readily among adults than in France.

Activité 7

Quand Léa et Axelle invitent Lou et Lucas à leur fête, elles utilisent 'tu' et 'vous'. Lisez leur conversation et expliquez pourquoi elles utilisent les deux façons de s'adresser à quelqu'un.

> – Salut!
> – Salut.
> – On voulait vous inviter à une fête chez Léa, samedi prochain.
> Lucas sourit.
> – OK, c'est cool.
> – T'es sur MSN?
> – Ouais.
> – Alors, donne-nous ton adresse, on t'enverra l'invit'!
> *(p. 207)*

Monsieur Marin speaks to his pupils individually using the *vous* form of the verb. This suggests a formal, old-fashioned and rather distant relationship between teacher and pupil. As adults usually use *tu* to speak to children, the teacher's use of *vous* suggests he sees his pupils as young adults whom he treats with respect.

When Lou first meets No she uses *vous* to address her. This demonstrates that Lou sees No as an adult who should be addressed politely. No, on the other hand, speaks to Lou using *tu*. She is not speaking to Lou as an adult would speak to a child, instead she is addressing her as an equal and trying to establish a connection with her. On their second meeting, Lou uses *tu* to talk to No. This demonstrates that Lou has started seeing her as a friend of a similar age to herself.

Activité 8

Pour chaque conversation dans cette liste, décidez si le personnage va utiliser 'tu' ou 'vous':

a) Quand No parle à Lucas elle dit…

b) Quand No parle à son assistante sociale elle dit…

c) Quand Lucas parle à Monsieur Marin il dit…

d) Quand Lucas parle à Axelle il dit…

e) Quand Lou parle à son père elle dit…

f) Quand Lou parle à ses parents elle dit…

Lucas, No and Lou at Lucas's flat, from the 2010 film adaptation

Informal language and slang

Lou's narrative is written in the colloquial language of a diary or spoken account. But she nonetheless writes in grammatically correct and sometimes rather poetic French. Her language is much more formal than that of No or Lucas. This is because Lou's account is written, whereas the words she reports from No and Lucas are always accounts of what they have said directly to her or to each other.

Lou uses direct speech to record the words of those around her. No speaks in very informal French: her use of **elision** and **slang** emphasises the informal nature of her communication.

> **elision** *l'élision (f)* when letters or words are removed from an expression to make it easier to say, for example: *j'ai pas vu mon père* instead of the grammatically correct *je n'ai pas vu mon père*, or *t'es adorable* instead of *tu es adorable*
>
> **slang** *l'argot (m)* the use of a non-standard word instead of the formal word. Common slang words in French include: *la bagnole* – car, *la clope* – cigarette, *les fringues* – clothes, *la thune* – l'argent

Tips for assessment

Elision is not acceptable in written French unless transcribing direct speech (as Lou does).

Activité 9

Dans la première phrase que No dit à Lou, '**– T'as pas une clope?**' *(p. 16)*, identifiez les exemples d'élision et d'argot.

No's lack of education and her marginalised position in society are reflected in her language. As Lou points out after their first meeting: '**elle n'était pas du genre à se formaliser sur la bonne éducation et tous ces trucs de la vie en société qu'on doit respecter**' *(p. 19)*. Lou's use of the informal *trucs* (stuff) in this sentence contrasts with the more formal *la vie en société*. The presence of two conflicting registers shows how Lou's way of speaking is influenced by No's frequent use of slang.

Lou gives her answer in correct, rather formal, French: '**– Non, je suis désolée, je ne fume pas. J'ai des chewing-gums à la menthe, si vous voulez**' *(p. 16)*.

Activité 10

a) Réécrivez cette réponse de Lou dans un registre moins soutenu: '**– Non, je suis désolée, je ne fume pas. J'ai des chewing-gums à la menthe, si vous voulez**'. *(p. 16)*.

b) Lisez cette liste de phrases dites par No. Pour chaque phrase, identifiez les exemples d'élision et d'argot. Ensuite, réécrivez les phrases dans un registre plus soutenu:

- **T'as pas une clope?** *(p. 16)*

- **T'as de ces questions! Y a pas de sens pour embrasser.** *(p. 105)*

- **Je suis pas de ta famille, Lou. C'est ça qu'il faut que tu comprennes, je serai jamais de ta famille.** *(p. 174)*

c) Ensuite, réécrivez la conversation à propos de la fête (activité 7 à la page 57) dans un registre plus soutenu.

Writing about language

Examining the kind of language with which a story is being told is always a useful way to understand what kind of story it is. In *No et moi*, it is vital, since our storyteller is also the main protagonist, and the way Lou expresses herself is closely connected to the sort of person she is. You might want to memorise a few examples of sentences that illustrate her personality through her storytelling style. These should illustrate not just what she says but how she says it. Consider also their impact on the reader:

- How do Vigan's language choices make the reader feel at key points in the novel?

- What effect does the use of language features such as colloquial expression have on the overall tone?

- How effective is Vigan's use of these features?

Vocabulary

s'adresser à (quelqu'un) to speak to (someone), to talk to (someone)

l'analyse (f) analysis

analyser to analyse

créer un contraste to create a contrast

le dialogue dialogue

éloquent(e) eloquent

s'exprimer to express oneself

le langage language (words used)

le narrateur / la narratrice narrator

la narration narrative

le point de vue perspective, point of view

le registre soutenu formal register

le symbole symbol

symbolique symbolic

le tutoiement the informal mode of address

tutoyer to use the *tu* form of the verb

le vocabulaire vocabulary

le vouvoiement the formal mode of address

vouvoyer to use the *vous* form of the verb when addressing one person

Useful phrases

Quand on considère... When we consider…

On trouve... We find…

Une analyse du langage révèle... An analysis of the language reveals…

Il devient de plus en plus évident que... It becomes more and more evident that…

On voit immédiatement... We immediately see…

d'une manière simple mais efficace in a simple but effective way

Nous constatons que... We note that…

Examinons le style du narrateur... Let us examine the narrator's style…

Sa façon de parler est... Her way of speaking is…

Son caractère / Son humeur s'exprime à travers son choix de mots. Her personality / mood is expressed in her choice of words.

Homelessness

Vigan's depiction of homelessness is powerful and moving. Unlike Monsieur Marin, Vigan does not just focus on the facts and figures. She gives us a comprehensive account of what it might feel like to live on the streets of Paris. By making No into one of the novel's main characters, Vigan can give the reader a detailed insight into her life. Vigan uses Lou's school project as a **plot device** to justify the long descriptions of life on the streets she includes in the novel.

Key quotation

Elle raconte la peur, le froid, l'errance. La violence. Les allers-retours en métro, sur la même ligne, pour tuer le temps [...].
(p. 60)

---

plot device *le procédé narratif* an event or character designed to enable a plot development in the story

Homeless women are particularly vulnerable. No tells Lou that men stare at her and try to follow her. She is frightened of falling asleep on the street in case something happens to her. Lou does not specify the dangers No faces, but the reader knows that homeless women like No are at risk of sexual abuse and even rape.

A woman sleeping on the street in Paris

Dehors, elle n'est rien d'autre qu'une proie.
(p. 63)

 Activité 1

Relisez les descriptions de la vie dans la rue *(pp. 63–66; p. 119)*. Imaginez que vous êtes un sans-abri. Rédigez une description de 80 à 100 mots d'une journée type. Utiliser le temps présent.

No's story clearly demonstrates that homelessness can happen to anyone. She describes the kinds of women she has met:

Key quotation

[...] des femmes normales qui ont perdu leur travail ou qui se sont enfuies de chez elle, des femmes battues ou chassées, qui sont hébergées en centres d'urgence ou vivent dans leur voiture, des femmes qu'on croise sans les voir, sans savoir, logées dans des hôtels miteux, qui font la queue tous les jours pour nourrir leur famille [...].
(p. 64)

Since Lou has met No, she pays much more attention to the homeless people she passes on the streets. Vigan uses Lou's descriptions of homeless people to demonstrate the extent of the problem to the reader:

Key quotation

[...] ils sont en groupe, chargés de sacs, de chiens, de duvets, ils se réunissent autour des bancs, ils discutent, boivent des canettes, parfois ils rigolent, ils sont gais, parfois ils se disputent. Souvent il y a des filles avec eux, jeunes, elles ont des cheveux sales, des vieilles chaussures et tout.
(p. 80)

Lou believes that she can help No. But other people are less convinced. Lucas has a bleaker attitude: '– On dit souvent que les gens qui sont dans la rue, ils sont cassés. Au bout d'un moment, ils peuvent plus vivre normalement' *(p. 121)*.

Vigan's depiction of homelessness includes a wide range of attitudes to it. She uses the woman who works at the kiosk in the *gare d'Austerlitz* to show how homeless people are seen as a problematic and unappealing group. She uses Lou's neighbours' reactions to the death of Mouloud to suggest that lighting candles for a dead man is much less use than helping him when he was alive would have been.

Lou criticises the way her neighbours leave candles at the spot where Mouloud used to sleep, even though none of them helped him while he was alive

In some ways, Lou represents the general public: she is naive and well-intentioned, yet she lacks any real knowledge of life on the streets. However, unlike her neighbours, Lou does try to help No. The fact that she fails suggests that Lucas and the social worker are right when they say that homeless people are hard to help. The detail with which Vigan depicts the everyday life of a homeless person helps the reader to look beyond their own misconceptions. We see that No did not end up on the streets by choice; she slipped through the cracks of a system which could not provide her with the love and support she should have received from her family. Vigan's novel shows not only that homelessness can happen to anyone, but also that homeless people are in danger of very quickly forgetting how to live the 'normal' life referred to by Lucas.

Tips for assessment

Upgrade

The contextual information you learned about earlier could be usefully drawn upon when discussing the central theme of homelessness in *No et moi*. For example, the French care system which ends support at age 18 meant that No found herself abruptly alone, with no family and few academic qualifications. If you were discussing the character of No or considering her homeless situation, this information could help you explain why she is in this situation.

Fear and courage

Lou makes frequent references to fear (*la peur*) in her story. At the beginning of the novel she is afraid of everything. But her friendships with No and Lucas help her to feel less scared.

> **Key quotation**
>
> **Je lui raconte combien j'ai eu peur, devant toute la classe, ma voix qui tremblait au début et puis après plus du tout, parce que c'était comme si elle avait été avec moi, comme si elle m'avait donné la force, […].**
> (*p. 103*)

> **Activité 2**
>
> Choisissez trois personnages qui ont peur dans le roman. Écrivez une phrase, dite par chaque personnage, pour expliquer de quoi ils ont peur.

Lou's friendship with No gives her the courage to try and change No's life. And Lou's bravery in turn helps her parents to leave their fear behind. When Lou's parents let No stay with them, Lou says: '**Il n'y a pas eu d'interrogatoire, pas de méfiance, pas de doute, pas de marche arrière. Je suis fière de mes parents. Ils n'ont pas eu peur. Ils ont fait ce qu'il y avait à faire**' (*p. 117*).

Social justice

Lou has a strong sense of social justice. She knows that No needs help and she wants to do everything she can to make her life better. But when Lou interviews No for the last time, she realises how powerless she is to help her: '**Et notre silence est chargé de toute l'impuissance du monde, notre silence est comme un retour à l'origine des choses, à leur vérité**' (*p. 61*).

> **Key quotation**
>
> **À partir de quand est-il trop tard? Depuis quand est-il trop tard? Depuis le premier jour où je l'ai vue, depuis six mois, deux ans, cinq ans? Est-ce qu'on peut sortir de là? Comment peut-on se retrouver à dix-huit ans dehors, sans rien, sans personne?**
> (*p. 68*)
>
> **[…] rien de tout cela n'a de sens, rien de tout cela n'est compréhensible, même avec le plus gros Q.I. du monde, je suis là, le cœur en miettes, sans voix, en face d'elle, je n'ai pas de réponse, je suis là, paralysée, alors qu'il suffirait de la prendre par la main et de lui dire viens chez moi.**
> (*p. 68*)

After her *exposé*, Lou feels increasingly guilty and ashamed about her failure to help No. The groups of homeless people camping out on the boulevard Richard Lenoir remind her of the gulf which separates her from No: '**Je les regarde avec cette honte sur moi, poisseuse, cette honte d'être du bon côté. Je les regarde avec cette peur que No soit devenue comme eux. À cause de moi**' *(p. 80)*.

Lou is deeply moved by the death of Mouloud and by the reactions of her neighbours. She finds it unfair that the owner of the café will adopt Mouloud's dog but that no-one will offer a home to a homeless person:

> **Key quotation**
>
> **Les chiens on peut les prendre chez soi, mais pas les SDF. Moi je me suis dit que si chacun d'entre nous accueillait un sans-abri, si chacun décidait de s'occuper d'une personne, une seule, de l'aider, de l'accompagner, peut-être qu'il y en aurait moins dans la rue.**
> *(pp. 81–82)*

The episode in which Lou stands up for Axelle in class *(pp. 126–127)* demonstrates her deep-seated sense of right and wrong. When Monsieur Marin pretends not to recognise Axelle after her haircut, Lou speaks up against him and is sent out of the classroom. This shows that her principles extend further than her concern for No.

Lou's bravery is manifested later in the novel when she continues to help No in secret: '**Nous allons nous occuper d'elle. Nous ne dirons rien à personne. Nous garderons ce secret pour nous tout seuls, parce que nous en avons la force**' *(p. 194)*.

'Les chiens on peut les prendre chez soi, mais pas les SDF' *(p. 81)*

Activité 3

Lou pense que No est à la rue parce qu'elle n'a pas su l'aider *(p. 80)*. Êtes-vous d'accord avec cette opinion? Écrivez un paragraphe de 100 à 150 mots où vous explorez les arguments pour et contre l'opinion de Lou. Qui ou quoi est responsable de la situation de No?

Secrets and lies

The **facade** that Lou presents to her teachers and classmates hides a family tragedy that she is not ready to talk about at the beginning of the novel. When Lou first meets No, she imagines that No is hiding a painful secret deep in her heart:

> **Key quotation**
>
> [...] sous l'empilement de ses trois blousons j'ai imaginé un secret, un secret planté dans son cœur comme une épine, un secret qu'elle n'avait jamais dit à personne.
> *(p. 20)*

This reference to a secret is an oblique reference to Lou's own family secret. Lou has not always been an only child. She had a sister, Thaïs, who died when Lou was eight. Lou cannot talk about the sudden death of her little sister with her parents and she keeps it hidden from her classmates and teachers. Sometimes Lou looks at the photographs of her sister which her parents have hidden away. These photos symbolise her memories of Thaïs which must also be kept locked away.

> **Key quotation**
>
> Ces moments ne nous appartiennent plus, ils sont enfermés dans une boîte, enfouis au fond d'un placard, hors de portée. Ces moments sont figés comme sur une carte postale ou un calendrier, les couleurs finiront peut-être par passer, déteindre, ils sont interdits dans la mémoire et dans les mots.
> *(p. 47)*

Activité 4

Il y a beaucoup de secrets dans ce roman. Choisissez trois secrets gardés par No, Lou ou Lucas. Pour chaque secret, écrivez une phrase pour expliquer pourquoi il faut ne pas le révéler.

facade *la façade* an outward appearance, especially a deceptive one

> **Key quotation**
>
> Certains secrets sont comme des fossiles et la pierre est devenue trop lourde pour la retourner.
> *(p. 157)*
>
> – Tu sais, Pépite, tout le monde a ses secrets. Et certains doivent rester au fond, là où on les a planqués. Moi, mon secret je peux te le dire, c'est que quand tu seras grande je t'emmènerai quelque part où la musique est si belle qu'on danse dans la rue.
> *(p. 159)*

After No starts working night shifts, she keeps her work-life secret from Lou. Lou's parents also want to protect Lou from learning too much about the kind of things No might be doing at work. They talk about No when Lou is out of earshot: '**Un soir je les ai surpris dans la cuisine, ma mère et lui, ils étaient en plein conciliabule, dès que je suis entrée ils se sont tus et ont attendu que je referme la porte pour reprendre leur conversation. J'aurais bien caché un ou deux micros sous un torchon'** *(p. 185)*.

In order to hide their secrets, the novel's characters spend a lot of time lying to each other and to themselves.

Lou's family are not very good at facing up to their problems. They would rather pretend that everything is fine than talk about their situation. This is illustrated by their attempt to have a 'normal' Christmas, even though they all know that Christmas has no meaning for them.

> **Key quotation**
>
> Noël est un mensonge qui réunit les familles autour d'un arbre mort recouvert de lumières, un mensonge tissé de conversations insipides, enfoui sous des kilos de crème au beurre, un mensonge auquel personne ne croit.
> *(pp. 84–85)*

Freedom, equality, fraternity

The motto of the French Republic is *Liberté, Egalité, Fraternité*. When we first meet Lou, she is naive and idealistic. She believes that she can change the world. But as she learns more about No's life on the streets she begins to realise that life is not fair.

> **Key quotation**
>
> Je pense à l'égalité, à la fraternité, à tous ces trucs qu'on apprend à l'école et qui n'existent pas. On ne devrait pas faire croire aux gens qu'ils peuvent être égaux ni ici ni ailleurs. Ma mère a raison. C'est la vie qui est injuste et il n'y a rien à ajouter.
> *(p. 102)*

In this quotation Lou questions the truth of the French Republican motto. She is beginning to realise the difference between ideals and reality.

Lou nonetheless believes that she can help turn No's life around. That is why she invites her to stay at her home and at first No's life seems to be getting better after Lou intervenes. But when No leaves Lou's home, Lou is once again forced to accept that life is not fair: **'il ne faut pas rêver. Il ne faut pas espérer changer le monde car le monde est bien plus fort que nous'** *(p. 191).*

Lou questions the truth of the *Liberté, Égalité, Fraternité* motto

Appearance and reality

Lou frequently refers to her own appearance. She looks younger than other people of her age and sees herself as tiny and insignificant. As we saw in the Language section, she often refers to herself as *petite*.

> **Key quotation**
>
> **Moi je n'arrive pas à grandir, à changer de forme, je suis toute petite, je reste toute petite, peut-être parce que je connais ce secret que tout le monde fait semblant d'ignorer, peut-être parce que je sais à quel point nous sommes de toutes petites choses.**
> *(p. 96)*

Activité 5

Pour chaque référence à 'petite' dans cette citation, écrivez une phrase pour expliquer ce que Lou veut dire. Ensuite, trouvez un synonyme pour chacun de ces sens de 'petit'.

But despite her small appearance, Lou is in reality capable of great acts. Vigan juxtaposes Lou's physical smallness with her moral greatness to show that things are not always what they seem.

As Lucas points out: **'T'es toute petite et t'es toute grande, Pépite, et t'as bien raison'** *(p. 121)*. Lou associates being *grand* with being brave: when she defends Axelle in class she says to herself **'je suis beaucoup plus grande qu'il n'y paraît'** *(p. 127)*. This comment could in fact be used to describe Lou's behaviour more generally. Lou looks childish and unimportant but in some ways she is the most significant character in the story. Not only is she the narrator, she is also capable of great acts which change lives.

Near the end of Section 8 *(p. 218)*, Lou notices an advertising hoarding which depicts a glamorous woman walking through a city at dusk. Lou compares this image with the sight of No walking away from her in the winter evening. This **juxtaposition** of illusion and reality symbolises the novel's attempt to look beyond surface appearance to the harsh realities which lie beneath.

> **Key quotation**
>
> Comment ça a commencé, cette différence entre les affiches et la réalité? Est-ce la vie qui s'est éloignée des affiches ou les affiches qui se sont désolidarisées de la vie? Depuis quand? Qu'est-ce qui ne va pas?
> *(p. 218)*

Characters, plot and themes

It can be helpful to think separately about the characters, plot and themes of the novel in order to explore each aspect of it in a systematic way. It is also a good exercise to explore how each one interacts with the other two. The American novelist Henry James once wrote: 'What is character, but the determination of incident? What is incident, but the illustration of character?' *(The Art of Fiction)*

In other words, James is saying that the point of characters is to drive the plot through their attitudes and behaviour, and the point of plot is to highlight characters through the ways they act and react. Each is in the service of the other.

In *No et moi,* we might say that Lou's belief in social justice is essential to the plot, as her refusal to give up on No leads to No moving in with her parents and finding the job in the hotel. At the same time, the plot of the novel serves to emphasise this trait of her personality by putting her in a situation where she can make a difference to No. We could also say that the theme of social justice is essential to both plot and character in the novel, and that both plot and character serve to illustrate this theme.

Consider whether there are any other characters, themes or plot developments from the novel that are dependent on each other and explore these in your revision.

---

juxtaposition *la juxtaposition* the placing of things or ideas side by side to highlight the differences between them

Vocabulary

avoir peur de to be afraid of

cacher to hide

coupable guilty

craindre to fear

la culpabilité guilt

explorer to explore

la force strength

grandir to grow up

la honte shame

impliquer to imply

l'impuissance (f) powerlessness

incarner to embody

la méfiance suspicion, mistrust

se méfier de to be suspicious of, to distrust

mentir to lie

le mensonge lie

s'occuper de to look after

prédominant(e) predominant, overriding

risquer de to be at risk of

signaler to indicate

suggérer to suggest

la ténacité tenacity

Useful phrases

Le thème est exemplifié par... The theme is exemplified by...

L'intrigue renforce le thème de... The storyline reinforces the theme of...

Ce thème est développé en... This theme is developed by...

Le thème de... est renforcé par les actions de... The theme of... is reinforced by the actions of...

... constitue l'un des thèmes principaux du roman. ... is one of the main themes of the novel.

Ceci est communiqué au lecteur par... This is indicated to the reader by...

Ce thème est étroitement lié à... This theme is closely connected to...

J'insisterai tout particulièrement sur le thème de... I will focus on the theme of...

Un épisode qui met ce thème en relief serait... An episode which highlights this theme would be...

L'un des thèmes principaux du roman, c'est... One of the main themes of the novel is...

Le thème est exemplifié par... The theme is exemplified by...

L'intrigue renforce le thème de... The storyline reinforces the theme of...

Ceci est signalé au lecteur par... This is indicated to the reader by...

Exam skills

Understanding the question

The exam questions will be written in French, which means there are two parts to understanding the question properly.

First, you need to ask yourself whether you understand the vocabulary, grammar and structure of the French in the question, so that you can be confident you have correctly understood its basic meaning.

Second, you need to ask yourself what the question is getting at.

- What are you being asked to do? Analyse, explain, compare?
- What kind of conclusion do you need to be heading towards, and what do you need to consider along the way?
- What material from the novel are you being asked to examine?
- What contextual material could you draw on to answer it thoroughly, for example, your knowledge of homelessness in France or the French school system?
- What approach should you take to your material? A character study? A for-and-against argument?
- What perspective(s) should you be considering? Your own personal view, or a more objective reader's view? A view that might be held by someone within the world of the story, or from outside it?

Vocabulary, grammar, and structure

If you have a choice of two questions, read both carefully. Make sure you have understood the French vocabulary correctly.

- Watch out for *faux amis*: *attendre* does not mean 'to attend', *blessé* is not 'blessed', *une déception* is not 'a deception' (they are 'to wait', 'injured' and 'a disappointment' respectively).
- Look too at the grammar and structure of the sentence. Is it clear to you how the various parts of it fit together?
- Even if they are separated in the sentence, you can see which adjectives go with which nouns, and which subjects with which verbs, through agreements.
- Pay attention to the relative pronouns *qui* and *que*. *La fille qui aide Lou* is 'a girl who helps Lou'; *la fille que Lou aide* is 'a girl whom Lou helps'.
- Look especially at verb forms to be sure you have understood tense, mood and active or passive constructions. There is a lot of difference between *elle aide* (she helps), *elle est aidée* (she is helped), *elle aurait aidé* (she would have helped) and *elle n'aurait pas été aidée* (she would not have been helped).

If you are unclear on the meaning of a word in the question, or confused by a grammatical construction, then there is a good chance you will still be able to work out the meaning of the question. Use what you *do* recognise in the sentence to work out the most likely meaning of what you *do not* know. You can also use your knowledge of *No et moi* to unravel the structure of the question.

In the end, though, answering a question without properly understanding it is a big risk to take. No matter how clever, well-researched and well-written your answer is, if it is not properly responding to the question that was asked, you will not gain marks. In a choice between two questions on *No et moi* it will always be best to pick the one you are more confident of understanding precisely, even if it is not a topic you are keen to write about.

Question types

Next you need to decide what approach the question is asking you to take.

Many questions will begin by asking you to examine (*examinez*), explain (*expliquez*), analyse (*analysez*) or evaluate (*évaluez*). In all these cases you are being asked to explore a topic in detail, including evidence from the text and using your contextual knowledge to demonstrate your understanding of the text.

In addition, *analysez* and *évaluez* are explicitly telling you that it is not enough to give information. You also need to interpret that information from your own point of view. That means you are expected to construct an argument for your own interpretation of the novel's meaning or your own judgment on the characters.

Note that, while *examinez* and *expliquez* do not specifically say that you also need to give your own interpretation and construct an argument to support your views, in practice you should always do this in an exam essay. Always analyse and evaluate, even if the question doesn't use those exact words. The Point, Evidence, Explanation (PEE) format can help you achieve this – when you make a point, support it with a quotation from the novel, then go on to explain and analyse its relevance to the argument you are making.

Other questions may ask 'What is the role…?' (*Quel est le rôle…?*), 'How far…?' (*Dans quelle mesure…?*) or 'In what ways…?' (*De quelle manière / façon…?)* What is the impact…? (*Quel est l'impact…?*). These questions draw attention to something else you should be trying to do in answering any question, which is considering the answer from different points of view.

Points of view

If you are asked what role a character (or, indeed, anything else) plays in the story, then there are several angles you can approach this from.

- You can look at it from the character's own perspective. What are their aims? How do they go about achieving them?

- Then move outwards a step and explore the perspectives of other people in the story. How do they feel about the character? What kind of relationship do they have with them, and how do they interact?

- Then step back further and explore the character from the writer's perspective. Why do you think the writer included them in the book? What role do they have in moving the plot forward? What themes do they help to illustrate? How do they throw light on the main character through interactions, similarities and contrasts?

- Finally, there is the reader's perspective. Is the character sympathetic? Do we identify with them, root for them, pity them? Or perhaps fear or hate them?

Similarly, if you are asked about the ways in which the novel does something (even if French prefers the singular 'in what way' – *quelle manière / façon* – to the English plural 'in what ways'), you are invited to look at several. As in the above example, you might look from the perspective of characters in the story, then the author, then the reader. Or, taking a different tack, you might examine the question with reference to the characters, then the plot of the novel, then the themes.

Often the best perspectives to use might simply be 'for' and 'against', as if arguing in a court case. When you are asked *Dans quelle mesure...?*, you are expected to examine both 'for' and 'against' in detail, and to reach a conclusion that doesn't necessarily plump for one side or the other.

Questions including quotations

Some questions will begin with a quotation (shown by double quotation marks "...") and then ask you to explain the extent to which you agree with the judgement / description / quotation: *Dans quelle mesure êtes-vous d'accord avec ce jugement / cette description / cette citation?* In this type of question it is important to begin by explaining what the quotation is suggesting, before presenting your arguments for and against.

Activité 1

Choisissez une question dans la liste de questions AS ou A Level à la page 81. Quels sont les mots les plus importants dans la question? Quels éléments du roman – de son intrigue, ses personnages, ses thèmes, etc. – connaissez-vous qui puissent vous servir dans votre réponse?

Planning your answer

You should take a few minutes of the exam to plan your answer before you start to write it. When you are revising, you might be tempted to plan lots of different possible answers and then try to memorise the plans. In fact, this could harm your answer on the day. Trying to make an exam question 'fit' with a pre-planned answer will waste valuable time and distract you from the focus of the question you should be answering. You may miss key elements or spend too long on a minor point.

Examiners are looking for essays that respond to the question that has been asked, precisely and in detail. That means you must understand the central elements of the novel. Become familiar with the text, its characters, language, plot, themes and context so that you can use the most relevant examples to support the points that you make in the most effective way. You must have thought carefully about all these things and developed your own opinions on them. You must also have written essays and essay plans, but do not try to learn the plans themselves. Instead, hone your skills at presenting your evidence and expressing your opinion on it in clear, elegant and accurate French. But what you need on the day of the exam is flexibility.

You need to be able to use your material flexibly to engage with the question that has been asked.

One of the most important – and most stressful – facts about essay-based exams is that, while revision and preparation are vitally important if you want to do well, you cannot have *everything* prepared in advance. The material you are going to draw on needs to be ready in your mind, but the way that you draw on it cannot be decided beforehand. It is true that the people who do best in the exam are usually those who have done the most careful and detailed preparation. It is also true, though, that success comes from a combination of preparation and intelligent use of your material on the day.

Two types of essay plan are explored on the following pages.

Linear plans

If you already have an idea of how the essay might be structured, you could use a linear plan to group your material under headings from the outset. Imagine you were answering the following exam-style question:

> Dans quelle mesure la gentillesse de Lou est-elle importante dans le roman?

A linear plan could look like this:

Gentillesse importante

Raison: La gentillesse de Lou permet à No de vivre en sécurité chez Lou.

Raison: La gentillesse de Lou permet à sa mère de s'occuper de No – son nouveau projet – sa dépression disparaît.

Citation: '[...] c'est une nouvelle vie qui commence pour elle [...], et moi je serai toujours là, à côté d'elle' (p. 117).

Gentillesse pas importante

Raison: La gentillesse de Lou ne suffit pas: il faut aussi que No réagisse.

Raison: La gentillesse de Lou, liée à sa naïveté, l'empêche de comprendre la réalité de la vie de No. Le rôle de Lucas est de dire la vérité à Lou.

Citation: '– On dit souvent que les gens qui sont dans la rue, ils sont cassés' (p. 121).

Autres choses qui sont importantes

Idée: Lou est guidée par ses principes: elle veut changer le monde.

Idée: Elle réagit aussi à un sentiment de solitude: elle veut avoir No comme copine.

Idée: Lou est aussi motivée par son travail scolaire; elle veut avoir une bonne note à son exposé: No est-elle exploitée par Lou?

Conclusion

La gentillesse de Lou est un élément-clé du personnage et on le retrouve derrière tous les événements du roman: très importante donc même si Lou ne parle jamais de sa propre gentillesse.

Spider diagrams

A spider diagram or a bullet point plan can help you to 'download' ideas without having a firm order in mind. You can jot down all the relevant points you can think of, then draw lines to connect them. This visual way suits some students more than others. Once you've drawn your plan, you can refine it, eliminating weaker ideas, combining others, then numbering your points to help you write up your plan in an ordered fashion.

A spidergram plan for the question on page 76 exploring Lou's capacity for kindness could look like this:

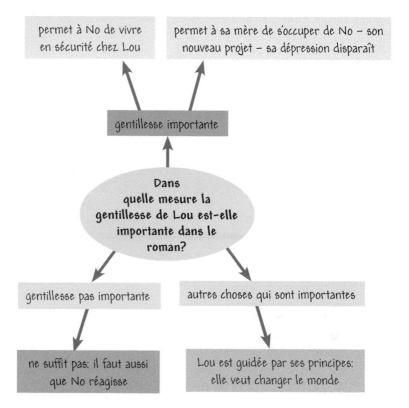

While it might be tempting to write your plan in English for speed, it makes more sense to do it in French. This way, you are already well on your way to having an essay expressed in good French: you simply need to expand on the points you already have. Also, writing your notes in French will make sure you do not get into the tricky position of making a point a key part of your argument, and then discovering that you do not know how to say it in French: this would make your whole essay fall apart.

Lastly, it is worth thinking about other angles that might provide useful material for the essay. Consider how the question looks from the perspective of other characters, the writer and the reader, for example.

Activité 2

Choisissez une question dans la liste de questions AS ou A Level à la page 81. Faites une liste ou un schéma en toile d'araignée de vos arguments en réponse. Quelles citations ou références au roman et à son contexte pouvez-vous utiliser à l'appui de vos arguments?

Writing your answer

Once you have your plan, you are ready to start writing your answer. Keep a rough idea in mind of how long you have, and how many words you are aiming for. Divide your time evenly between the number of sections you want to write. If you are writing an essay with a for-and-against argument structure, then you ought to be allowing around half your time for the introduction and first part, and half your time for the second part and conclusion. If your essay involves a wider approach, count the number of points you want to make from your plan, add the introduction and conclusion and divide your time roughly between each of them.

It is very easy for an examiner to see when an essay is unbalanced because a candidate has spent too long on the early parts and then rushed the conclusion – or not even got to a conclusion at all. It is also quite easy to make sure you do not get into this situation, if you are careful with your time. Practise writing timed essays in exam conditions so you get a sense of how much you need to do in the allotted time.

While you cannot have your whole argument prepared in advance, you can have a stock of French expressions stored up, which you can call on in order to present your material within a structured argument. The list at the end of this section (page 80) provides you with some examples.

Using quotations effectively

A quotation can be a good way of providing evidence for the point you are making. It is more precise than a paraphrase and, if you have a quotation that relates closely to the argument you are making, there can be no stronger evidence for your case than the words of the author herself. When looking for quotations to memorise, always start with an idea of a point you might want to make in an essay, then go looking for the right quotation to back up that point. There is no point in learning a quotation unless you know exactly how you might use it. Even better, find a quotation you could use in several different essays, with relevance to more than one argument you might be making.

Do not memorise more of a quotation than you need to. If the evidence you want for your point is contained in three or four words, there's no point in memorising more. It will only take up more of your writing time, and you will not get extra credit for it.

Using Point, Evidence, Explanation

While you do not have to stick to it rigidly, the well-known formula for structuring paragraphs, Point, Evidence, Explanation (PEE), is just as useful for essays in French as in English. Consider the following exam-style question examining the importance of Lou's kindness in the novel.

> Dans quelle mesure la gentillesse de No est-elle importante dans le roman?

Here is a paragraph taken from a sample student's response to this question.

The student makes a clear statement in answer to the question.

They give evidence for their viewpoint by referring to the events of the story.

They strengthen their evidence with a short quotation from the text, which they link to their point.

Bien que Lou soit motivée par sa gentillesse, il ne faut pas oublier ses autres motivations. Il est évident que Lou veut réussir à l'école. Elle invite No au bar uniquement pour la persuader de lui raconter son histoire. L'idée d'inviter No chez elle vient beaucoup plus tard. Lou passe beaucoup de temps à se demander comment elle va 'convaincre No de m'aider'. Le témoignage de No est essentiel pour la réussite de l'exposé de Lou. Cela suggère qu'au début de son amitié avec No, Lou est motivée par son travail scolaire. Lorsqu'elle commence à comprendre la vie de No, sa gentillesse la pousse à l'inviter chez elle.

The student finishes their paragraph with a clear explanation of how the quotation and the events of the story reveal that Lou's behaviour was not initially motivated by kindness, but that her kindness came later and led to No's rescue.

Upgrade

Tips for assessment

A successful answer will provide evidence of your ability to:

- demonstrate perceptive understanding of theme, character setting and literary techniques
- respond confidently to the question asked
- make points in an ordered way and use well-chosen evidence to support them
- write in accurate and expressive French, demonstrating a good variety of vocabulary and sentence structure.

Understanding the different levels of the story will help you develop perceptive and thoughtful responses to the text. On the surface, it is the story of a lonely young girl finding friends unexpectedly and growing from these friendships. On a deeper level, it is a commentary on the plight of the homeless, which invites the reader to question what should be done. You must show an understanding of how both these things work together and are important for the success of the novel as a whole.

Useful phrases

To introduce your argument:
D'abord…; Premièrement…; À première vue…; Je commencerai par la question de…;
Je parlerai tout d'abord de…; Pour commencer…

To link a series of points together:
D'abord…, ensuite…, enfin…; Premièrement…, deuxièmement…

To introduce a new subject:
À propos de…; En ce qui concerne…; Il est important / nécessaire / essentiel de noter que…;
N'oublions pas que…; Quant à…

To give an example:
notamment; par exemple

To give an explanation:
autrement dit; c'est-à-dire

To explore both sides:
D'un côté…, d'un autre côté…; D'une part…, d'autre part…; D'un point de vue…, de l'autre point de
vue…; Il est vrai que… mais…

To explain why:
parce que; puisque; à cause de

To give an opinion:
à mon avis; quant à moi; personnellement

To argue an opposite view:
cependant; par contre; néanmoins

To express frequency:
d'habitude; de façon générale; des fois; en général; fréquemment; régulièrement

To concede a point:
bien que + subjunctive; en dépit de

To sum up:
pour résumer; en somme

To conclude:
pour finir; ainsi, pour conclure; en guise de conclusion

Sample questions

AS

1

Examinez la vie de No avant qu'elle arrive chez les Bertignac.

Dans votre réponse vous pouvez considérer les points suivants:

- l'enfance de No   • l'importance de Loïc et Geneviève   • sa vie dans la rue.

2

Examinez les similarités et les différences entre Lou et Lucas.

Dans votre réponse vous pouvez considérer les points suivants:

- la vie scolaire   • leur situation familiale   • leurs rapports avec No.

3

Expliquez l'importance de l'exposé de Lou.

Dans votre réponse vous pouvez considérer les points suivants:

- le sujet de l'exposé   • les interviews avec No
- la réaction des élèves et de Monsieur Marin.

4

Expliquez les rapports entre Lou et ses parents dans le roman.

Dans votre réponse vous pouvez considérer les points suivants:

- l'effet de la mort de Thaïs sur la famille   • la vie à la maison au début du roman
- comment les choses changent après l'arrivée de No.

A level

1

« Dans *No et moi*, Vigan montre une société cassée, égoïste et hypocrite. » Dans quelle mesure êtes-vous d'accord avec ce jugement?

2

« Lou est une narratrice problématique: le lecteur ne peut pas lui faire confiance. » Évaluez à quel point cette description de Lou est justifiée.

3

Analysez comment Vigan représente la situation des femmes dans le livre.

4

Dans quelle mesure peut-on décrire *No et moi* comme un roman optimiste?

Sample answers

AS sample answer 1

> Expliquez comment Delphine de Vigan représente la vie des SDF dans le roman.
>
> Dans votre réponse vous pouvez considérer les points suivants:
>
> - les témoignages de No   • l'amitié de Lou pour No   • la mort de Mouloud.

Un SDF (sans domicile fixe) est une personne qui vit dans la rue. En France il y a beaucoup de SDF. Dans *No et moi*, Delphine de Vigan décrit la vie des SDF de plusieurs façons. Tout d'abord, elle utilise l'exposé de Lou pour expliquer le problème. Afin d'aider Lou, son professeur, Monsieur Marin, lui donne des statistiques. Alors que ces données montrent l'étendue de la situation, les témoignages de No sont plus frappants parce qu'elle décrit des situations que nous pouvons imaginer. Elle parle de la faim, de la peur et du froid.

Ensuite, les descriptions que Lou donne de No soulignent les effets néfastes de sa vie dehors: 'cette amertume à ses lèvres, cet air de défaite, d'abandon'. Cette citation montre que No souffre de façon physique et de façon émotionnelle. Le lecteur partage l'amitié que Lou a pour No parce que nous la connaissons grâce à Lou. Nous sommes donc touchés par son histoire. En outre, Vigan raconte d'autres histoires à travers les mots de Lou et No. No décrit la vie de plusieurs femmes qu'elle rencontre à la rue et Lou parle de la mort de Mouloud.

D'une façon générale, Vigan se sert des expériences de No et des réactions de Lou pour nous donner une vision complète de la situation des SDF à Paris. En guise de conclusion, on peut dire que le rôle important joué par No dans le roman invite le lecteur à s'identifier avec sa situation. Ainsi, comme dans l'exposé de Lou, ce livre rend visible une situation trop souvent oubliée par le grand public.

Marginal annotations:

Useful to explain the term and situation the context. Would be better to include an actual figure instead of *beaucoup de* which is too vague.

Good use of connectives throughout (*tout d'abord, ensuite, en outre,…*).

An appropriate point about the *exposé* which is then supported with an example (the figures from Monsieur Marin).

The student continues with an evaluation of the effectiveness of the figures and a suggestion that No's testimony is more effective: excellent use of the PEE structure.

Would be better to give specific examples rather than only talking about how Vigan gets homelessness into her novel.

Excellent use of quotation: not too long, relevant and very well analysed to show the different levels of No's suffering.

Thoughtful reference to the effects of Lou's friendship on the reader: demonstrates that the student appreciates that this is a work of fiction.

Very convincing conclusion: the parallel drawn between Lou's *exposé* and the novel itself is clever.

This is a very good essay: it demonstrates in-depth knowledge of the text and of the theme of homelessness. It focuses on how Vigan uses the novel to discuss homelessness and shows several techniques used by the author to make the reader feel differently about the subject. It does not retell the plot or include descriptions of homeless people, and it avoids unnecessary waffle. Instead it concisely shows how the characters of No and Lou function to communicate the facts of homelessness in an emotive way. The essay is well-structured and has a thoughtful and clever conclusion.

AS sample answer 2

> Expliquez les rapports de Lou et No dans le roman.
>
> Dans votre réponse vous pouvez considérer les points suivants:
>
> - leur première rencontre
> - la période que No passe chez Lou
> - le départ de No.

A strong first sentence which establishes that the initial focus of the essay will be on the paradoxical nature of the girls' friendship.

Appropriate, specific reference to the novel to provide evidence; also demonstrates attention to style.

This list of actions is too descriptive; it just retells the novel's plot without giving any analysis. Student needs to explain what these actions mean for the relationship between No and Lou.

Tout d'abord, nous pouvons constater que les rapports de Lou et No sont caractérisés par un paradoxe: alors que No est plus âgée que Lou, c'est plutôt Lou qui se comporte en adulte. Lors de leur premier rencontre à la gare, Lou vouvoie No. Cela suggère que Lou voit No comme une adulte. Ensuite, Lou et No sont sur un plan d'égalité. Elles parlent ensemble et No aide Lou avec son exposé. Lou veut être l'amie de No mais No vit à la rue donc elle disparaît. Dès que Lou retrouve No leurs rapports changent: malgré la jeunesse de Lou elle devient métaphoriquement plus 'grande' que No. Elle prend la décision d'accueillir No chez elle. Cela montre que No redevient enfant et Lou s'occupe d'elle. Ce rapport métaphorique mère-fille est souligné par la présence de la mère de Lou qui redevient mère pour s'occuper de No.

Good to make a reference back to the theme of *petite / grande*: this shows that the student is thinking about the novel and its language on several levels.

Useful to bring in the reference to Lou's mother; a shame that Lou's jealousy is not also mentioned here.

En deuxième lieu, nous allons examiner le thème de la confiance dans le roman. No demande souvent si elle peut avoir confiance en Lou. Paradoxalement, à la fin du roman, c'est No qui trahit Lou en l'abandonnant à la gare. Cela montre que leur amitié n'est pas assez forte pour sauver No. Alors qu'en apparence No et Lou sont amies, le fait que No laisse Lou à la gare suggère que l'assistante sociale avait raison: les gens de la rue ne sont pas fiables. Le comportement de No montre que les rapports de Lou et No sont harmonieux en apparence, mais un mensonge en réalité.

Helpful 'signposting' sentence to the next theme, although the use of *en deuxième lieu* seems odd given that this is the final paragraph of the essay. A reference to the word *rapport* from the essay question at some point might have helped.

Good idea to bring in the theme of appearance and reality.

Needs a concluding sentence relating all points made back to the question.

This essay does a good job of relating the question to several of the novel's key themes. It sometimes includes plot description, but also uses references to key stylistic effects and important moments. The focus of the essay appears to wander away from the question at times; this student may well have prepared material on key themes and then tried to get it into an essay where it doesn't really fit.

A Level sample answer 1

> « Dans *No et moi*, Vigan suggère que les valeurs républicaines de liberté, égalité et fraternité n'existent pas dans la France contemporaine. » Évaluez dans quelle mesure ce jugement porté par le roman est justifié.

Strong introduction: responds to the question and announces the main direction of the argument.

'Liberté, Égalité, Fraternité' est la célèbre devise de la république française. Dans *No et moi*, Vigan dépeint une société où il est difficile de trouver ces valeurs.

Effective use of quotation.

The whole of this paragraph demonstrates very good use of the PEE structure: a point is made, examples are given and then the examples are evaluated.

Premièrement, l'égalité n'est pas très apparente dans le livre. Comme le dit Lou: 'On ne devrait pas faire croire aux gens qu'ils peuvent être égaux, ni ici, ni ailleurs'. Prenons la scolarité de Lou et No à titre d'exemple. Alors qu'en principe tout le monde peut aller à l'école jusqu'à l'âge de 18 ans en France, No a quitté l'école à 15 ans sans diplômes. Elle n'a aucun soutien familial donc elle n'est pas aidée dans ses études. Par contre, les parents de Lou peuvent lui acheter des livres et un ordinateur. Elle va bien réussir à l'école grâce à son intelligence et sa situation familiale aisée. La différence entre Lou et No montre un manque d'égalité.

A good idea to use paragraph openers (such as *Premièrement*, *Deuxièment*, *Troisièment*) to indicate the three parts of the argument: this makes the essay structure very clear.

Deuxièmement, la liberté manque aussi dans le livre. No n'a pas de responsabilités mais elle n'est pas libre pour autant. Quand elle loge au centre elle doit rentrer avant 19 heures. Sa liberté est limitée parce qu'elle n'a pas d'argent, pas de travail et pas de chances dans la vie.

Cependant works very well here to announce a change in direction. This is a clever twist in the argument.

Troisièmement, le fait que No se trouve à la rue indique un manque de fraternité: ses concitoyens ne font rien pour l'aider. Depuis qu'elle est toute petite No est abandonnée par le système. Cependant, le roman n'est pas complètement dépourvu de fraternité. Le personnage de Lou représente cette valeur républicaine. Lou veut aider les gens qui en ont besoin. Elle veut combattre le manque d'égalité et donc de liberté dans la société. Sa générosité envers No et la façon dont elle s'inquiète pour elle nous montrent que la fraternité, ou plutôt la sororité, existe encore.

This conclusion is convincing because it refers to the three values and then brings in the author, thus demonstrating that we are reading a book. The parallel between Vigan and Lou is insightful.

Pour conclure nous pouvons dire que Vigan aussi fait preuve de sororité en écrivant le livre. Comme Lou elle veut dénoncer le manque d'égalité ou de liberté dans la France actuelle.

This is an excellent essay. It has a well-controlled and carefully articulated structure and every point it makes is backed up by a specific reference to the text or a quotation from it. It includes a twist at the end which captures the reader's attention and makes us think about the novel in a different way. It demonstrates good textual knowledge and the ability to analyse and think independently.

A Level sample answer 2

> Analysez comment Vigan représente le thème du mensonge dans *No est moi*.

French a little basic; could replace with
qui ment de la façon la plus évidente.

No et moi est un roman réaliste qui décrit la vie des SDF avec honnêteté. Paradoxalement, il y a aussi plusieurs types de mensonges dans le livre.

Tout d'abord examinons les mensonges racontés par un personnage aux autres personnages. No est le personnage qui ment le plus. Elle invente l'histoire de Loïc et elle cache les détails de son travail à l'hôtel à Lou et Lucas. Lou, par contre, ne dit pas de mensonges, mais elle ment par omission quand elle ne dit pas à ses parents que Lucas vit tout seul.

Ensuite, il y a les secrets. Sans mentir explicitement, la famille de Lou garde la mort de Thaïs sous silence. Lou ne peut pas en parler avec ses parents. Cela a des effets néfastes qui montrent qu'il est dangereux de mentir. Leur secret crée une distance entre Lou et ses parents. Elle n'aime pas quand ses parents font semblant d'être normaux alors qu'ils cachent un secret. Lou utilise le vocabulaire du théâtre pour montrer que sa mère fait semblant d'être une bonne mère alors qu'elle est en réalité très distante.

Vigan souligne la présence des mensonges dans le roman pour mettre en question la fiabilité de sa narratrice. Puisque nous savons que Lou ment par omission, il faut se demander si nous pouvons lui faire confiance en tant que narratrice. Lou ne ment pas au lecteur comme No, mais elle ne comprend pas toujours ce qu'elle raconte. Elle parle de l'argent de No sans se poser de questions. Elle donne au lecteur des indices qu'il doit comprendre lui-même.

Pour conclure, il y a plusieurs types de mensonges dans le livre. Vigan suggère ainsi que nous vivons dans une société mensongère qui projette une réalité qui n'existe pas vraiment.

Interesting introduction: would be strengthened if the main direction of the argument was mentioned; it would also help to mention the various types of lies.

Good start. Use of *tout d'abord* suggests a logical structure and use of *examinons* draws the reader in.

Not quite accurate: she invents the letters.

Excellent reference to Lou's language.

A clever reference to the narrator – this lifts the essay and stops it being merely a list of different kinds of lies.

Thought-provoking conclusion which makes a link between one of the novel's themes and Vigan's intention in writing the novel itself.

Add something here to increase fluency: *Ensuite, il ne faut pas oublier les secrets cachés qui sont également une forme de mensonge* would be better.

This essay gets better as it goes along. At first it feels like a rather flat list of different kinds of lies. The references to the narrator and then to Vigan's intentions show that the candidate is thinking about how the theme of lies relates to the novel as a whole. It is a shame that the points made in the final paragraph and the conclusion were not mentioned earlier, perhaps in the introduction. The paradox of the truthful depiction of homelessness could have been more clearly discussed in the body of the essay and perhaps referred to again in the conclusion in relation to Vigan's intentions. There are also some parts where the language is a little simplistic and more advanced structures could have been used.

Exam question translation

AS *(page 81)*

1

Examinez la vie de No avant qu'elle arrive chez les Bertignac.

Dans votre réponse vous pouvez considérer les points suivants:

- l'enfance de No
- l'importance de Loïc et Geneviève
- sa vie dans la rue.

Examine No's life before she arrives at the Bertignacs' home.

In your response you could consider the following points:

- *No's childhood*
- *the importance of Loïc and Geneviève*
- *her life on the streets.*

2

Examinez les similarités et les différences entre Lou et Lucas.

Dans votre réponse vous pouvez considérer les points suivants:

- la vie scolaire
- leur situation familiale
- leurs rapports avec No.

Examine the similarities and differences between Lou and Lucas.

In your response you could consider the following points:

- *school life*
- *their familial situation*
- *their relationships with No.*

3

Expliquez l'importance de l'exposé de Lou.

Dans votre réponse vous pouvez considérer les points suivants:

- le sujet de l'exposé
- les interviews avec No
- la réaction des élèves et de Monsieur Marin.

Explain the importance of Lou's presentation.

In your response you could consider the following points:

- *the subject of the presentation*
- *the interviews with No*
- *the reaction of the other pupils and of Monsieur Marin.*

4

Expliquez les rapports entre Lou et ses parents dans le roman.

Dans votre réponse vous pouvez considérer les points suivants:

- l'effet de la mort de Thaïs sur la famille
- la vie à la maison au début du roman
- comment les choses changent après l'arrivée de No.

Explain the relationship between Lou and her parents in the novel.

In your response you could consider the following points:

- *the effect of the death of Thaïs on the family*
- *life at home at the beginning of the novel*
- *how things change after the arrival of No.*

A Level *(page 81)*

1

« Dans *No et moi*, Vigan montre une société cassée, égoïste et hypocrite. » Dans quelle mesure êtes-vous d'accord avec ce jugement?

'In No et moi, *Vigan shows us a broken, selfish and hypocritical society.' To what extent do you agree with this judgement?*

2

« Lou est une narratrice problématique: le lecteur ne peut pas lui faire confiance. » Évaluez à quel point cette description de Lou est justifiée.

'Lou is a problematic narrator: the reader cannot trust her.' Evaluate the extent to which you agree with this statement.

3

Analysez comment Vigan représente la situation des femmes dans le livre.

Analyse how Vigan represents the situation of women in the novel.

4

Dans quelle mesure peut-on décrire *No et moi* comme un roman optimiste?

To what extent can we describe No et moi *as an optimistic novel?*

AS *(page 82)*

Expliquez comment Delphine de Vigan représente la vie des SDF dans le roman.

Dans votre réponse vous pouvez considérer les points suivants:

- les témoignages de No
- l'amitié de Lou pour No
- la mort de Mouloud.

Explain how Delphine de Vigan represents the life of the homeless in the novel.

In your response you could consider the following points:

- *No's testimonies*
- *Lou's friendship for No*
- *the death of Mouloud.*

AS (page 83)

Expliquez les rapports de Lou et No dans le roman.

Dans votre réponse vous pouvez considérer les points suivants:

- leur première rencontre
- la période que No passe chez Lou
- le départ de No.

Explain the relationship between Lou and No in the book.

In your response you could consider the following points:

- *their first meeting*
- *the time which No spends living with Lou*
- *No's departure.*

A Level (page 85)

« Dans *No et moi*, Vigan suggère que les valeurs républicaines de liberté, égalité et fraternité n'existent pas dans la France contemporaine. » Évaluez dans quelle mesure ce jugement porté par le roman est justifié.

'In No et moi, *Vigan suggests that the republican values of freedom, equality and brotherhood do not exist in contemporary France.' Evaluate the extent to which this judgement of the novel is justified.*

A Level (page 86)

Analysez comment Vigan représente le thème du mensonge dans *No est moi*.

Analyse how Vigan represents the theme of lying in No et moi.

Answers

Plot and structure

Activité 6 (*page 12*)

a3, b7, c1, e8, d10, f4, g2, h5, i9, j6

Activité 10 (*page 17*)

connaissais – imparfait; avais – imparfait; m'étais installée – plus-que-parfait; distribuait – imparfait; s'est tourné – parfait; a souri – parfait; étaient – imparfait

Activité 12 (*page 19*)

1. The chronological order in which events are experienced:

a4, b8, c12, d15, e2, f20, g5, h16, i22, j1, k10, l18, m3, n7, o17, p21, q13, r6, s9, t19, u14, v11

2. The order in which they are recounted in the novel:

a6, b2, c11, d15, e4, f20, g7, h16, i22 , j3, k10, l18, m5, n9, o17, p21, q13, r8, s1, t19, u14, v12

Language

Activité 7 (*page 57*)

The party invitation is extended to both Lou and Lucas, which is why 'vous' is used initially. However, since Lucas accepts the invitation (and Lou doesn't respond), Léa and Axelle switch to 'tu' as they begin talking just to Lucas.

Activité 8 (*page 58*)

a tu, **b** vous, **c** vous, **d** tu, **e** tu, **f** tu (when speaking to one of them) vous (to both together)

Glossary

arrondissement *l'arrondissement (m)* a section of central Paris: Paris is divided up into 20 *arrondissements*, rather as London is divided into boroughs such as Westminster and Chelsea. The lower the *arrondissement* number, the closer it is to the centre of Paris

baccalaureate *le baccalauréat (le bac)* exam taken at the end of secondary school, equivalent to British A Levels

bildungsroman *le bildungsroman* a German word (also used in French and English) for a novel which describes the emotional and intellectual development of a hero, usually as they move from childhood or adolescence to adulthood

chambermaid *la femme de chambre* a maid who cleans bedrooms and bathrooms in a hotel

colloquial expressions *le langage familier* informal words or phrases, more commonly used in spoken language

day centre *le centre d'accueil de jour* a place where homeless people can go to use the computers and look for work

denouement *le dénouement* the story's resolution

depression *la dépression* a mental condition characterised by feelings of severe despondency and dejection, typically also with feelings of inadequacy and hopelessness

elision *l'élision (f)* when letters or words are removed from an expression to make it easier to say, for example: *j'ai pas vu mon père* instead of the grammatically correct *je n'ai pas vu mon père*, or *t'es adorable* instead of *tu es adorable*

emergency shelter *le centre d'hébergement d'urgence a* state-funded centre which provides short-term accommodation – dormitories and showers – for homeless people

empathise with someone *s'identifier avec quelqu'un* to understand someone's point of view or to feel a connection with someone

facade *la façade* an outward appearance, especially a deceptive one

first person narrative *le récit à la première personne* a story told from the perspective of a narrator speaking directly about himself or herself, using the pronoun 'I' / *je*

high school *le lycée* where French students go usually between the ages of 15 and 18. The first year is known as *seconde*, the second year is *première* and the final year is *terminale*. Lou and Lucas are in *seconde*

hypocrisy *l'hypocrisie (f)* claiming to have standards while not actually living up to those standards

l'Île-de-France Paris and its surrounding area; people who live here are known as *Franciliens*

imagery *les images (fpl)* visually descriptive language which conveys ideas or emotions

interior monologue *le monologue intérieur* a speech carried out by one person inside their head

insomnia *l'insomnie (f)* problems getting to sleep or staying asleep

juxtaposition *la juxtaposition* the placing of things or ideas side by side to highlight the differences between them

naive *naïf / naïve* showing a lack of experience, wisdom or judgement; childlike or innocent

narrate *raconter* tol tell in a story-like format

narrator *le narrateur / la narratrice* person who is telling the story

narrative voice *la voix narrative* the voice of the person who is telling the story

plot device *le procédé narratif* an event or character designed to enable a plot development in the story

protagonist *le / la protagoniste* the central character in a story

redoubler to repeat a school year a second (or third) time because it wasn't passed the first time round

register *le registre linguistique* the level of formality used in communication

reintegration shelter *le centre d'hébergement et de réinsertion sociale* a state-funded centre where a person in great need of help can live while trying to find a job and complete administrative procedures

repetition *la répétition* the repeating of a word or phrase, often used to add emphasis

retrospective account *le récit rétrospectif* a description of events in the past which is told with the benefit of knowledge gained since the events happened

retrospective narrative *le récit rétrospectif* a story in which the narrator describes events looking back from a point in time after the end of the story has been reached

slang *l'argot (m)* the use of a non-standard word instead of the formal word. Common slang words in French include: *la bagnole* – car, *la clope* – cigarette, *les fringues* – clothes, *la thune* – l'argent

suburbs *la banlieue* district on the outskirts of a large city. Although wealthy suburbs exist in France, the word *banlieue* often implies an area of poverty and social exclusion

utopian *l'utopiste (m / f)* an idealist, a dreamer

OXFORD
UNIVERSITY PRESS

Great Clarendon Street, Oxford, OX2 6DP, United Kingdom

Oxford University Press is a department of the University of Oxford. It furthers the University's objective of excellence in research, scholarship, and education by publishing worldwide. Oxford is a registered trade mark of Oxford University Press in the UK and in certain other countries.

British Library Cataloguing in Publication Data

Data available

ISBN 978-0-19-841835-1

Kindle edition ISBN 978-0-19-841827-6

10 9 8 7 6 5 4 3 2

Printed in Great Britain by CPI Group (UK) Ltd, Croydon CR0 4YY

Acknowledgements

The publisher and author would like to thank the following for permission to use photographs and other copyright material:

Extracts from *No et moi* by Delphine de Vigan © Editions Jean-Claude Lattès, 2007

Cover: Alex Linch/Shutterstock; **p7, 20:** AF archive/Alamy Stock Photo; **p22:** PJB/SIPA/REX/Shutterstock; **p24:** Ditty_about_summer/Shutterstock; **p25:** Akaiser/Shutterstock; **p27:** Harriet Hadfield/Shutterstock; **p30, 34:** AF archive/Alamy Stock Photo; **p38:** ALEXANDER KLEIN/Getty Images; **p41, 44:** AF archive/Alamy Stock Photo; **p53:** ivanmateev/Depositphotos; **p54, 58:** AF archive/Alamy Stock Photo; **p62:** 2p2play/Shutterstock; **p64:** milli/iStockphoto; **p66:** Tramino/iStockphoto; **p69:** funlovingvolvo/123rf.

Every effort has been made to contact copyright holders of material reproduced in this book. Any omissions will be rectified in subsequent printings if notice is given to the publisher.